THE
WORDS
Of
MY LIFE

CHRISTINA MARRA

BALBOA.
PRESS

A DIVISION OF HAY HOUSE

Balboa Press books may be ordered through booksellers or by contacting:

Balboa Press
A Division of Hay House
1663 Liberty Drive
Bloomington, IN 47403
www.balboapress.com
1 (877) 407-4847

Because of the dynamic nature of the Internet, any web addresses or links contained in this book may have changed since publication and may no longer be valid. The views expressed in this work are solely those of the author and do not necessarily reflect the views of the publisher, and the publisher hereby disclaims any responsibility for them.

The author of this book does not dispense medical advice or prescribe the use of any technique as a form of treatment for physical, emotional, or medical problems without the advice of a physician, either directly or indirectly. The intent of the author is only to offer information of a general nature to help you in your quest for emotional and spiritual well-being. In the event you use any of the information in this book for yourself, which is your constitutional right, the author and the publisher assume no responsibility for your actions.

Any people depicted in stock imagery provided by Thinkstock are models, and such images are being used for illustrative purposes only. Certain stock imagery © Thinkstock.

Print information available on the last page.

ISBN: 978-1-5043-5855-2 (sc)
ISBN: 978-1-5043-5856-9 (hc)
ISBN: 978-1-5043-5868-2 (e)

Library of Congress Control Number: 2016908452

Balboa Press rev. date: 08/08/2016

For my son Michael, who has showed me what it means to truly love with everything that is in me and with all that I am.

For my parents and my siblings. And of course my grandmothers.

For my cousin Rick.

For B.

I often write of love or sadness
Words flow from my heart
To escape the inevitable feeling
The endless stories of my soul
Are recounted here in black and white
Like footsteps on damp sand
Each emotion scarring my soul
Each word written comforting it
And still I am writing
An attempt at keeping a small piece
Of each of life's inspirations
I always find you here
Listening to my thoughts as
They sound out triumphantly
And like the notes of orchestra
My song lingers
And I find myself hoping it will be caught
By you.

Chapter 1

*I*t begins. Just like that. The journey to self. Like the brightness of moment, lightning strikes and I am born. A new meaning, a new path, a new thought.

I breathe. I am.

Just like that it happens. Life is born with the first of breaths inhale. I am born. I exist. I think and am and feel.

Life surrounds me. Chaos surrounds me. I live a life of chaos. And so it continues...

From the moment a child is born, the conditioning begins. Think this, learn that, commit this to mind, to memory, to heart. Begin the study of the automatic chains of reaction that come from years of tending.

Like lost sheep, there is a following. Quietly guided by the gentle hand of Shepherd.

I grew up then. I opened my eyes. I saw. Did you? I may have. One cannot be sure. When does one really see?

I notice the development of conscious thought, and more frightening than that, unconscious and random ideas.

When did I truly begin, I wonder? When did my once guided movements take a violent shove to independent condemned effort?

I often filled my mind with the brilliance of long before Wonders. Wonders I can only hope to be part of, as my soul lives on, as theirs do, on the shelved existence of greatness.

Yards of thoughts take shape on blank pages of possibility as I share with you the development of me.

You do want to know me, don't you? Why wouldn't one be interested in the natural progression and development of another… Perhaps another that somehow reminds of oneself. I must be like you. I must think like you. There must be some connection to a shared existence. I know we have shared thoughts.

We must be because we share. We share many things. Not only am I, but are we. We relate; our thoughts and our words. I feel it every time I read or write a passionate thought on existence. I feel your life before me.

I look back on the innocence of soul. Like the stretching of kittens paw I was awakened. Expanded to take in all that surrounds me. One cannot express the sensation of expanding soul.

I am growing.

Tiny hands grasp the largeness of comforts palm. Can you hear him? Can you feel the whiteness of new emotion finding its way home? This is home. At least, I hope it is.

Large eyes look up at me, catching my loving gaze. What magical moments will follow the rhythm of this child. And so it begins. Just like that it happens.

He is. He was before I noticed. But, nonetheless, he is. Right here, demanding attention. He has been heard.

Soft scents of pastel realities overcome me. The gentle sound of murmured music to my ears; an endless sea of indescribable emotions… Overwhelming hope, and dreams, and love surface. Warm breath rises against midnight clouds while echoing sounds of lullabies cast shadows on nursery walls. Tiny fingers grasping adult hearts luring constant craziness into the incredible intensity of perfection.

I was a child once. I vaguely remember. Growing up in sheltered existence, I began. I remember thinking. I remember crying. I remember pieces of magnificent moments etched in my mind. Will these moments remain with me? Will I hold them forever?

Time went on, as did I. I found myself circling the reality of my being. Even a child finds moments of inquisitive mind. But what peacefulness… what calm. What natural ability to love and hurt and feel with no remorse, no fear, no anxiety, no discord.

And so it happens...The development of mind. New thoughts penetrate a once free soul, forcing the hand of Thought. I fell in love with him, you know? Thought, I mean. He encompassed my being. He lured me. Here I find myself, constantly ravelled in the chaos of him. The chaos I call life. My life. Welcome home. You will stay awhile, won't you?

How unique it is. My life, I mean. How wonderfully 'only mine' it is. I spent years hiding from the nature of my soul, trying to find the road where I turned wrong. I haven't now, have I? I am just where I am supposed to be. Here. Right here, in your hands. Hold me closer. Just for a moment or two.

I remember learning in school. I remember the smallness of it all. How large it all seemed once, in the eyes of Innocence. Innocence is growing. What direction she follows is still unclear, or is it?

My parents were strong teachers. They groomed me from birth. They still do. Snip here, trim there… Like a small puppy I was 'learned' the consequence of gesture. The slight of hand and nod of head can still enchant me… Push me, if you will, into the direction of pre-determined fear and greatness.

Here is where greatness begins. Conditioned from birth we trudge along. We find ourselves waiting on tense moments casting future direction. Future direction that follows the footsteps drawn out by long ago paths gone astray. Paths that are looking for retribution.

Well, not my path. After all, it is only partly mine.

I woke up one day and found myself a bright-eyed adolescent. Everything I found, I touched. The texture of life enticed me. It still does. I learned the touch, the sensation, the feel of emotion. I watched it grow. I felt it. I reached out and touched the intensity of Emotions heart.

Long flowing hair protected me…Similar to the enchanting tone of mermaids' song. One could not hurt or bruise such a free soul as mine. I was nearly invincible. Sometimes I still think I am. Then a burst of reality, and I am enlightened.

Somewhere inside myself, I knew I was frightened. My constant desire to understand more, a defense against worldly things unknown. Like all things undefined, I was challenged. Pulled slower, held back, restrained by any possible means to slow the progression of revelation. I appreciate that now. I was allowed to feel the vibrations of life just long enough to recognize the different 'feels.' Just long enough to recognize before being violently thrown off of the spirit of Matador's bull.

There was unreigned effort and passion in every movement. There was a constant flow of energy filling me with an insatiable desire for more. I still find it hard to control. I came to know the exhaustion that followed the constant movement of mind and soul and being. There are some things so dear to me though, that I could only embark on, and appreciate, while on the last string of Energy's guitar. It is in these moments of near exhaustion that I see my true self, feel my true emotions; understand my true devotions.

I do love, you know. Not just me, but you as well. I always did. I wish you had seen me sooner. I would have loved to travel with you. Assuming you were heading in my direction, of course. Would you have modified your path to accompany mine? I always was interested in the depth of one's emotion, and their willingness to change form.

I started writing at this point. I recognized my appreciation of emotion. I noticed others and the expression of theirs. I wanted to reach out each time I saw the movement of exchanged expression of any kind. I found myself drawn to music and words and quiet exchanged glances of hidden desire. I captured them. I still have them you know? I keep them locked in a secret room in my soul. I find odd comfort in recounting them… the chase that led me to hold the mystic wonder of Real.

And what lies within? Perhaps a stubborn assertive spunky personality… slowly emerging into a world of craziness… Searching for the me of who I am. I find myself sitting here… staring at the pearly skies… Waiting for your mind to meet mine.

How does one put faith in the warmth of the day when
it is so easily cooled by the coming of night?

How can one learn to fear the flame of fire when it
can be sizzled with the intense wetness of rain?

How does one enjoy the comforts of life when
we are so often reminded of death?

How can one give into the euphoria of love
when it is so often followed by pain?

How does one begin?

Chapter 2

*L*ife has a funny way of unfolding itself. Feelings are here and gone the next. Relationships come, change, and go. The foundations of our existence turn upside down with one turn of the dice. All the while we struggle to maintain some kind of certainty, some level of comfort, some on-going security.

I have found that over the last ten years of my life, things have been anything but consistent. Well, they've been consistently inconsistent, if that counts for anything. I have had my heart broken at least once, I have broken two hearts that I am aware of, I have experienced two life changing, monumental events, and I have seen many others experience life disappointments. I have seen confidence and trust lost, and I've seen empires of effort rise and fall.

Somewhere along the way, society has accepted the changing circumstances of their lives and have attributed the awry-ness of it all to *times changing*. I suppose there is some truth to that. Life really does go on. No matter how hurt, or disappointed, or joyful one is, tomorrow always comes. Most times a blessing in disguise. At least tomorrow does come…

In times of immense emotion of any kind, I am surprised at the ease in which tomorrow arrives. Business demands focus, family, friends, and loved ones, demand attention. It seems sometimes, that there is not a moment in between. The time for reflection has been lost… along with the desire for one to reflect. One must make a conscious effort to stop long enough to sigh, look back, learn, and carry forward. Hopefully stronger, smarter, and armed for the next roller coaster of emotions that tomorrow's life will bring.

We have all lost and gained in our lifetimes. Romantic love, familial love, or platonic love, have entered and exited most of our lives, bringing with them, good and not-so-good times. *Not to mention longstanding business partnerships…*

Almost every kind of relationship has some common goal of success, whether long term or immediate. Each kind of relationship brings us to a new level of understanding. Yet what hesitation to let it end if it is not taken away from us, that is, with circumstances beyond our immediate control.

At what point is it leaving too soon and at what point are we holding on too long? I wonder if there is a silent relationship's standard that screams out to us when we are straddling the line of life's next step. We decide every day. We dress, we work, and we stop. All pre-determined actions, and yet when faced with life choices we falter, we hide, and we push back and sometimes regress. We compromise what means most to us as individuals for what means less. Is it driven by fear? A cowardice that surfaces with the unsure step forward and what our life choices may bring? In stepping forward we find our strength. We find our way. Armed with this knowledge we still shrink back with fear. Some do. Others face the fear and ultimately the consequences of their choices. Good or bad. No matter which path we take the result will be the same. Time does not stop the path we are meant to walk, it just slows it. When we are enlightened and self-aware, pushing forward to that facing of reality is less fearful. I am happy that I am not afraid.

I am afraid of many things, but not moving forward. I am not afraid to find my way.

In my attempts to find consistency in an inconsistent environment, I have found this instead. Life isn't entirely about what or who is in your life, it is more about what you learn and bring forward to your new day, hopefully as a result of those partnerships. Life isn't always about winning, as a matter of fact, I think sometimes, I'd rather lose. Life isn't about keeping love, it is about letting love enhance your life and bring you closer to your goal of everlasting happiness. Love doesn't always bring happiness. I have learned, that most times, it brings strain. What is great about life is that, no matter what happened yesterday, the promise of tomorrow never ceases to shine. Tomorrow's possibilities and realities truly heal today's pain. There comes a time when one must ask themselves, if I am not happy with the accomplishments of today, what do I really have, but the hope of what tomorrow may bring?

Chapter 3

W hat I love about emotion is the constant reminder of actual. I always liked things defined. I still do. I find definition more difficult now. Not every adult is ready to have things so clear. Not every adult is an adult. Mirrored images are not always as they really appear, or as we would like them to, for that matter. Have you noticed that? When did you last see me? When did you last see you? I notice every day. Well, at least, I try to.

Chaos. Tension. Surrounding moments of craziness. Difficulty, tragedy, wasted efforts. Aggravations. Existence.

I begin my career. And what a spiral it is… upward I wonder? Parts of me have come so far. Parts of me have yet to open and unfold. It seems that I have not slept for what feels like an eternity. Restless nights and frustrating days… fatigue overwhelms me. Reality has become a dream as confusion sets in around me. Shaded days filled with pastel thoughts and a forever-ness of vacant words. Blank pages of unfinished half thoughts drape my desk in whiteness. Tomorrow is invited by Today's incomplete tasks leaving me frazzled. I look forward to an eternity of organized craziness. Family Business.

I never noticed, as I was growing up, how quickly time seemed to pass. As a matter of fact, I am <u>still</u> growing up, and it is only recently that I have come to realize how quickly the days seem to end.

I wake up in the morning, *late as usual*, begin the mad frenzy of getting ready for work, only to begin my day at the office with one less working hour as a result of my insatiable desire for sleep. The day is a whirlwind of organized chaos, *the story of my life*, ending somewhere around six as I make a mad dash to my evening meetings.

Sometime around nine thirty, my workday ends. I rush out to see my friends, family, boyfriend, half exhausted, and barely able to breathe. The night ends at midnight. I make my way home to find the comfort of my bed waiting for me. What would be nicer would be having the sheets already warmed, awaiting the familiar shape of my body.

The endless ringing and hustle bustle of our everyday life leaves us with no time to enchant ourselves with dreams and child-like fantasies. The world around us is so political and crude. I am a part of it - aren't I? Could it be possible that once leaving the academic "scholarly" years, that the mind ceases to grow?

Careers lead to routine, which leads to laziness of the mind, yet academics lead to boredom and mental exhaustion. Is there no in-between? Is expanding as a person wrapped in a series of moments and experiences that challenge who we are and what we do?

Is it solely in living that we expand? The growth that only comes from life experience? Does happiness happen when this knowledge is attained? Do we reach a peak and accept that if this is it, if this is all I will become, it will be enough? Is the constant search for all things greater our minds way of saying that we are not enough? Is it in experience and education that we find the ultimate acceptance? The acceptance of self? What will it take before we see ourselves as perfect and worthy and enough?

When is it that one really knows what one wants? How could one individual distinguish what makes one truly happy? Is ultimate happiness even possible?

One is happy in love. One is happy with friendship. One is happy with achieved successes.

Life brings happiness along with pain, anger, and joy. Who says when these feelings are and what you experience is which feeling? My happiness could equal your jealousy, or my sadness could lead to your joy. Who really decides what is felt? If emotions lead to knowledge, how does any person know what another has felt or how knowledgeable one is?

I suppose that no one cares. With all the hustle and bustle of everyday life, who really has time to worry?

I wake up once more, *earlier this time*, rush into the office, glance at my Palm Pilot (Yes, Palm Pilot – I'm how old?) and notice that the week that follows carries the same theme as the last…. **FULL**.

I stop for a second as I enjoy my morning coffee, check my e-mail, begin my daily routine… I am thinking about time.

How quickly it passes you by. I sometimes feel as if time consumes itself before it even begins. The day ends before the sun comes up and the week is over before Monday ever comes. Before I know it, another month is gone, and before long, I am celebrating the beginning of a new year. Each time I reflect on my past years accomplishments, the joys, the sorrows, the goals I have achieved, and my newest aspirations.

The vicious cycle will begin again.

I wonder if life will ever slow down. *Surely once I get married*… of course, then I'll be rushing home to spend time with my life partner, laundry, house-keeping, gardening… a new routine of craziness will set in. Perhaps I will have more time when I have children… of course, then I'll have my career, a husband (and all that comes with being a wife), I will need extra time and energy for the children… playing, colouring, teaching, *learning*…. then come the beginnings of family routine… the comfort platform each parent provides for their child... regular meal hours, healthy meals, story time, play time, family time. Notice how there is no mention of MY TIME? Does my time end as responsibility increases? How does that work exactly?

Does increased domestic and professional responsibility equate loss of oneself?

Each stage of life has its probable trials and tribulations, not to mention its constant demand for attention. Still, there will never be more hours in a day. Time will never slow so that I, among many, can have that extra hour of sleep that I so desperately require.

Today I have decided to slow down. I now ask myself, where do I begin?

Chapter 4

C ircumstance creeps up on me, tackling me when I least
expect it, leaving me weary and bruised to the bone…
fatigued beyond the most intense of tiredness.

When I finally gain my strength and rise to my feet, I find
misfortune offering me a hand; staring back at me like my own
reflection in this morning's mirror.

I once thought life's conditioning had purpose… now I find
myself wondering if some higher power has a skewed sense of
humour. Life laughs at my deepest pains, whipping stones against
the weakness of my sentiment, constantly challenging my strength
of will, breaking me in the process, piece by piece until I finally
look up, aching and insignificant, pleading to keep what is left of
my sanity.

I am stripped of pride and the comforts of stability, once
again returning to the rockiness of turmoil. Fear consumes every
area of my life; my rationale, my efficiency, my ability to love.
I find myself hiding the realness of my soul, terrified of being
discovered, seeking refuge in the craziness of routine.

Each wound burying another part of my soul… leading me
down the familiar road of ruin… a loss of one's way, a loss of
ones' happiness, a loss of oneself.

Yet through each moment of weakness I find a new level
of strength, raising me up and padding me once again for the

inevitable fall... a roller coaster of unstable emotions governing the existence of my being.

Through each new platform of fatigue, I am renewed, infused with unsought-after greatness, ever-learning, ever-growing, ever-experiencing.

Through every sadness, every happiness, every sorrow, I have given thanks that I have been able to feel. Perhaps that higher power has a plan after all. I suppose I have yet to learn.

And then a new world begins. The grandness, the realness, the splendor. I am lost in foreign dreams of warmth and cool, and the final realization of comfort. Endless thoughts race and minds reel with excitement. The anticipation of long sought after perfection.

Clouds of love burst above me, showering me with damp affection. What magnificent moments unfold and fill this instant. Words cannot describe the incredible opportunity... a world awaiting discovery. I wait anxiously in anticipation of my future.

A world of new beginnings. I am living on my own.

There is something magical in newness. Beginnings are wonderful. Like sunshine ignites the fire of spring, I am uplifted. I once dedicated a poem to new beginnings. The start of all things comes with such intensity. The anticipation of a probable success or possible failure...

The excitement that comes hand in hand with not so distant dreams created in the heart of my mind. The shadow of fear cast over seeming possibilities racing forward with frightful exhilaration. All the while, I find myself, envisioning the culmination of my desire....

Like the coming of storm before rainbow's magnificence, dreams are conquered by destiny. A magnificent battle, as fated plans roll out like the rage of thunder.

Past faux pas and long ago future paths are cast away by the brightness of this moment. A ray of light; a shift in perception; a bright focus. The brilliance of New.

Blankets of whiteness cover the new walls of my life. Strong vibrant beating drums echo into my coming reality. Soft green pastel shades invite moments of glimmering comfort as I enter into the soothing sound of your familiar voice.

Hallways of emptiness surround me mirroring drastic moments in my life, and with each new dusting of magic, the beginning of bright horizons dawn.

Constant patter of falling rain washing blueness off today's wounds, while smiling faces hide behind unknown doors.

The cleansing of the days grayness has been captured by the splendor of this evenings star.

The tranquility here is so inviting. I find myself wrapped up in a soft towel of comfort. The evenings chill is pale in comparison to my newfound warmth as my thoughts drift to him. I am in love. How pleasant it is to have the shadow of your being dance to the whispering chirp of evening's leaves. Heavy clouds hang above me, engraving the blackness of the sky, something like the sound of your voice echoing endlessly in my mind. The wonder of your distant smile like the hidden moon, masked behind a wall of dark… mysterious and out of reach and then bright and brilliant inspiring the magic of stars. And then in an instant, I am back in this moment, enjoying the tranquility of new.

Chapter 5

I remember looking forward to long walks under the evening's moon… always accompanied by the warmth of a hand and the familiarity of laughter. *I still do.* There is something so *warming* about the comforts of partnership.

What is in a partnership? There is the undeniable feeling of belonging that makes even the worst of problems seem that much less severe. There is the affection level and all that comes with it; the intensity of passion, the confidence of boosted egos, the unmistakable feeling of being loved. There is the loving. Not just 'that' loving, but the loving of another.

My favourite part of partnership would have to be communication. I love exchanges of emotion. Have you ever noticed how one word can drastically change any given moment? The right word spoken (or written, for that matter) can set an atmosphere of romance, and the wrong word can lead to one of your most draining of arguments.

So here you find yourself, wounded by the intensity of words, all the while, your partner, seemingly on the opposite end of battle's field, hangs on lingering emotions, wrapping them in trusted arms. *The battle has begun.* It is not long before stained armour finds its rightful home and painful exchanges leave open wounds of heartache. Somewhere amidst the bloodshed of anger, a white flag is raised marking the end of masquerade.

You seek a post and *lick your wounds,* all the while being followed by the softness of anger's retreat, wrapping you in a cloth of unexpected understanding. Raised walls come tumbling down as tears of fatigue drown moments of irritation. The storm has passed and your partner remains. Quite the same as you found them earlier, *only gentler this time.*

This exchange of words opening one more door of soul; a passageway to the innermost feelings of the one you love.

There is nothing greater in the universe than being understood. The culmination of love...*truly being seen.* Not in the formal sense of how you walk or wear your hair, but in the truest sense of *vision.* Beyond the smile and frown and nervous laugh, right into the heart of who you are. The deepest scar of your most recent pain, your softest weakest moment hidden beneath walls of insecurity, masked by years of surreal confidence... your deepest fear, your craziest dream, your hopes, your goals, your desires.

Here you find yourself, partnered with seeming perfection... looking over at you from across the room, reaching into the very heart of who you are, watching you with a gaze so intense that it encompasses your entire being. Every ounce of your realness is observed, *and hopefully accepted.*

This acceptance, the foundation of partnership's comfort, bringing you to a new level of strength. Strength that leads you to a new depth of love... In this love and mutual admiration, a true romantic partnership is formed. From this partnership begins your life... all beginning with the warmth of a familiar hand under the haze of an evening's moon.

I think I am in love...and then again...and then Again. The names change, but the relationship stays the same. Together we find ourselves, lost amidst a sea of dream...Far away from the elements of reality; the routine of chaos, work, friends, and family. Here we are, surrounded in the tranquility of countless moments of happiness. Waves crash under the paleness of the moon. Glistening eyes gaze fondly marking the beginnings of love...

I awake to find myself a girlfriend. A new world begins. The whirlwind roller coaster of emotion brings me to a new level of height and drops me back to my knees in one magnificent blow... comparable only to the feeling of growing fear and anticipation in my stomach as the dropping of roller coasters' momentum off mountains edge.

Twinkles of softness caress me as I look into love's eyes. Sweet sensations gliding over soft lips and warm hearts sending vibrations of comfort up my spine. Handheld walks under perfect skies lead me down foreign roads of Happiness as I fall into the calmness of perfection's embrace.

Heated moments of passion circle over the quietness of new love and I am left captivated. Like the clearing of morning haze I feel brilliant. The comfort of tranquility.

I find myself carried off in the gusto and wonder of seeming love, only to open my eyes, much wider this time, and find myself wrapped in a distorted vision of jaded truth.

Through it all I see him. The faceless image of all I hope to be with. He is magnificent. He challenges me on every level, forcing me out of my chosen destiny of routine. I paste him onto every love I find, and then in an instant, I am aware, I have once again followed an uncertain path of empty happiness.

In every seeming love, I find myself in relationships chaos. The disapproving family, mine or his own; the two paths that never seem to merge, and quite often go astray; the intimacy that fulfills the immediate desire, but never beyond. I close my eyes and drift, coasting along until the crash of wave turns me over, reminding me that I must begin again. This time, I should not lose me along the way. This time I should continue me, and nurture us.

The seeming love will begin again.

In a society filled with text messaging, email, loose to little meaning on valuable, endearing words, how does one find substance? Where does one find a person who is not afraid to stand apart from the herds and love out loud? How does one who stands alone find comfort with one who cannot?

Who is my Shepherd? Who is his? My parents were my shepherds once, holding me back from my naïve wildness, trying to put boundaries on the me of who I am. I was never content being a sheep. At another point my teachers confined me...In a scholarly way of course. I am not a sheep anymore. I refuse to be herded. Perhaps the reason I find myself in a current state of lonely. I will follow my dreams into the unknown.

I think I am in love again. This time I know it is seeming. Standards change, expectations change, acceptance is mandatory, and society will not settle for less. Why would they? After all, technology's conditioning has left us with a society lacking substance. Social skills begin to decay, and I find myself wondering how many genuine individuals are in my world. The faces I choose to surround myself with. A world that is entirely my own. A world I am fully responsible for creating.

Mountains of desire build up within me and every part of me aches for him. Walls of security crumble as I enter the uncertainty of emotion. Fear is born within me on this cool autumn night and I consume myself with endless thoughts of timed constraints.

I want to hide from what may come to be and land safely in the craziness of routine. Visions of solitude conquer moments of passion and I am torn. I am somewhere between love and the possibilities of heartache.

Perhaps it is not seeming love am I trying to avoid. Perhaps it is genuine hope and acceptance that I seek.

Love itself is a wonderful thing. For as long as I can remember I have loved almost everything. I love to work... a lifestyle choice, not a sickness. I love to play and the innocence that comes with it.

I love the tempo of music. I love to relax and couch-cuddle and be warm. I LOVE the sound of laughter. I love the comfort of hugs. I love the belonging of family and I love the *overwhelmingness* of love. I love children.

The thought of any of the above sends my heart into a whirlwind of happiness; picking me up in all of its gusto and sweeping me into the sweetness of calm.

What I love most about emotion is comfort. I find comfort in the hurt of each pain, the joy in each happiness, and the sadness of each loss. Somehow I *find myself* in the depth of emotion.

Writing, for instance is my perfect example of this. I have been writing for as long as I can remember. I am incapable of expressing myself on paper when life becomes constant. In order to release my 'creative mind' I bring conflict into my life. I need highs and I need lows... *neither of which are drug induced...*

My deepest emotions surface with instability. After periods of constant I find myself overwhelmed with bottled sentiment. Looking for an escape I create a pattern of conscious turmoil. Imagine this for an instant. Self-inflicted turmoil. Whose image of *goodness* was I made in?

Having said all of this and completely losing myself in the intensity of words, I bring you back to love. I love my ability to be completely taken by joy and then find myself completely pensive, in brief and consecutive instants.

If love were a combination of emotions, comfort would have to be my favourite. Comfort is warm and safe. Comfort is the first cry of life from your newborn child. Comfort is the security of a mother's embrace after your first skin-breaking fall. Comfort is knowing that each night, after even the most lengthy, draining argument, you will wake up to find the one you love.

I love to feel... mostly *loved.*

Intimacy, one of the most beautiful aspects of love, can be summed up in one word. Well, maybe two. *Utterly incredible.*

The sensation itself is fabulous, but apart from that, the *feeling* is completely overwhelming. Not only in the formal sense of feeling, but emotionally speaking.

The comfort and closeness that come along with both the physical and emotional aspects of intimacy, in my opinion, drive a relationship. What I cannot understand is why so many couples complain about the change in their intimate relationships upon entering into the institution of marriage. Why does a higher form of commitment change the level of closeness one wants or needs to feel with their partner?

Part of my *(and I am quite positive, the young generation's)* fear about marriage, is waking up to realize I entered into a *seemingly* lifelong commitment only to find myself alone. Bringing me to my next point. What makes one want to get married?

Is this a normal progression in life or an issue of status quo? When does one realize that "the time" has come? Is it a result of convenience or truly driven by love? *Is* there a one true love? *I used to believe there was...Would I be naive to say I still do?*

I always thought that I would find perfection. Not in the literal sense of the word, but someone who was perfect for me. *In my experiences with dating to date*, I have learned that there IS NO perfect mate. In my opinion, there is absolutely NOT one person who can meet ALL of another's needs. Perhaps this is why it is so easy to find comfort outside of one's marriage (or relationship). Perhaps the stereotype of *the mate that fulfills you in every way* gives young people, like myself, a false belief in the reality of what married (partnered) life really is. Even when you have chosen your "perfect" mate, there is still a need for outside companionship, *of the opposite sex or otherwise*, to pick up the slack of what your partner does not emotionally or intellectually provide.

Here is the hard part...the part that involves integrity, strength of character, and discipline. NOT letting the *other* "friendships" go further than what they are. A mutual need for additional companionship or mental stimulation. What I cannot understand is why maintaining boundaries has become such an issue for so many people in today's society. At what point does an outside friendship, strictly platonic, emotional companionship, take a violent shove into some light level of intimacy? One may argue this issue for hours I am sure. I could have a single-minded debate on this myself.

I am an adult. I have had boyfriends that I cared about a great deal. We were always fairly close in age, we had fun together, and we enjoyed laughing, arguing, and debating. However, I still felt the need for the bonds that I have developed over the years, with both my male and female friends. Contrary to popular belief, there are people in this world who respect the "commitment" aspect of their commitments. Similar to my ability to follow the law as an abiding citizen, is my ability to follow my strong value system (thanks to mom for that... a strictly regimented moral code of conduct was instilled in me from infancy), which, as an aside, still governs my personal life. Values that were instilled in me since childhood. *Perhaps even before then.*

With all due respect to modern-day parenthood, could it be possible that the reason our rate of failed relationships is so high, has nothing at all to do with a young generation *gone astray...* but a young generation with fewer instilled values?

Perhaps the problem has something to do with the *value* one places on intimacy and not the *level* of intimacy at all. I wonder if such a fast-paced society has time to place value on emotions as intense and positively enveloping, as intimacy. Have we become intimately illiterate?

Then I think of the years that will pass and all that they may bring me... countless moments of happiness, sorrow, pain, and ecstasy. Before long I will awake, ring on my finger, child in my arms. The gifts of love that will be brought to me through Marriage.

Just like that it happens. I realize why I want to marry. **For love. For companionship. For family.**

I ache for closeness. For the touching of skin and the softness of lips, and for the vision of soul.

I ache for warmth. Yours and my own. The moment that follows the igniting of passion and the fire that burns away old wounds and old scars.

I ache for the magic. The awe of the unknown and the spark that ignites the flame.

I ache for passion. The intensity of combined energy, the softest touch on yearning skin. The coming together of mixed desires; the racing, beating hearts that follow instincts climax.

I ache for the first meeting.

I am revisiting this area of my book many years later. Since then I have been married, had a child, separated, and found love again. I've put the wrecking ball through my life again only to lead me to focus on finding me.

When I read about one person being unable to fill all of our needs I would still agree today. But not in the same way. I do believe that one person can meet all of your romantic and companionship needs and not leave you feeling unfulfilled. That is possible. It was for me. And although it was briefer than I would have wanted, it was true, and pure, and all encompassing.

There is danger in straddling the line of temptation. And when you are unhappy or unfulfilled, any amount of attention or love can lead you to believe that your temptation is real. The standard you are willing to accept is lower, and you may find yourself accepting less than what you ultimately want, but more than you are currently receiving.

We have a natural tendency to develop attachment to people in our lives. Even people who are 'just friends.' These attachments can threaten a relationship depending on the level of attachment.

At any point when your chosen partner is not the first person you call for comfort, you are being faced with a red flag of an underlying issue. And if the person you do rely on for comfort is of the opposite sex, and is attractive to you, in any way, it could lead to other developments.

Relationships require boundaries that both parties can find happiness within. Relationships are based on agreements made with our chosen partner. The importance of respecting those agreements in our loving, is paramount and will make or break a union.

We all have our non-negotiables. Things we cannot live with, and cannot live without. Finding a way to incorporate, compromise on, and in some ways, pacify the needs and insecurities of both parties, in my opinion, will ultimately be what solidifies your union.

A partnership should leave you feeling safe and protected. A place where you can love and err openly and without judgement. You need intimacy to have the passageway and pathway to meaningful love and sex. And if we stop making time for the intimate opportunities that life presents us with when in our relationships, we slowly break down the safe, protected feelings that we achieved in our relationships' infancy.

People often talk about lack of sex in marriage. I often wonder if the sex is prefaced by holding hands, eye contact when talking, and random gentle touches during the evening. The loving that leads up to the loving that we want later.

Why do we not take the time to ensure that we are in a relationship where both people are similar in how we assign feelings and values to what means most to us?

Chapter 6

I salivate as hunger pains burn within me. Triggered by a moment, a touch, a glance.

The flames of cooped up silent images surround me. I have nowhere to run and nowhere to hide. My pulse races as cold beads of sweat cool the intensity of combined auras.

The magnitude of forces towering over me as the tempo of beating hearts merge. I am fighting. I am yearning. I have been conquered by desire.

When I see redness, I think of him, in all of his vibrance and passion, all that makes up the painful him. I watch him as he sleeps at night; the gentle way his chest moves against the rhythm of his breathing... Red. I watch him as he drinks his coffee; holding his mug with a rough tenderness... sipping slowly as the steam masks his face... Red. I watch him as he dresses, his hands making slight movements from button to button and then one drastic movement as he zippers his pants... Red.

I watch him as he smiles at me. I hear the softness of his voice. I feel the passion in his touch. As he slowly comes towards me, I see all he is and all he makes me, all the brightness in his eyes, all his movements. I see him.

I see all that makes up what he is to me. Words do not describe how I love Red.

The gentle sound of the breeze cools the racing beat of my heart. The softness of the chirping birds leaving me peaceful and content. Lights dimmed and distant rays pause to catch the beauty of the moment. A solitude of magnificent forces sending fluttering branches into ecstasy.

The warmth of the beating sun sending chills up my spine, as I bask in the chosen darkness. My mind whirling, my body aching. The anticipation of seeing you again.

Like a gust of wind he takes my breath away. The clouds hang dark and heavy above me in his absence. They mark the emptiness I feel. The moisture lingers in the air like the faint smell of cologne after a long nights' romance. He returns. With a sudden radiance, he shines on me. He brings me warmth and comfort in his closeness. Emotions are stirred. The storm that was looming has passed. Counted moments of happiness.

My stomach aches with desire. My being yearns to hold him. His soft skin brushes against me as the summer breeze amuses.

His caresses are soft and sweet, stirring emotions of joy, of love, of lust. Feelings circle within... I feel a deep burning passion. Can you hear it? And then as if ever-awaited, a sudden burst... A release of pain and hunger and softness.

A cool shudder as his heart beats with mine. To begin again reminds me of the endless intensity of him.

When I think of chemistry, I think of him. His bright eyes burn into me and his smile penetrates my soul. Desire lingers on every part of my being as my mind wanders to thoughts of him. Playful moments and forbidden games entice me and I find myself lost in a sea of dream.

Endless reasons keep me distant while hunger pulls me near. A confusion of mixed thoughts whirl around me and rationale finds no home.

I am entirely captivated by the essence of him.

And then I am waiting. I am not sure what I am waiting for. Is it the coming of dream or the return of comfort? Either would bring me my sought after exhilaration.

I find myself thinking of him. Who exactly is he? Where does he come from? He has a shape in my mind. He has a persona. I wonder sometimes if he really exists. I wonder all of the time… perhaps he is my soul's wish on paper. Sometimes I think he is a piece of everyone who has touched my life.

Mostly I see him in romance…watching me from across the haze of love. He sends my heart racing, exciting me in an instant. The brightness of his eyes, melt me. I always feel his warmth, even when I am miles away from his embrace. There is consistency in his absence. I sometimes wonder if he's *ever* been there.

He is the object of my dreams. He is the love I am waiting for. He is the love I desire. He sees me, beyond it all. I *know* he does. I know he is close to me, yet not yet touching my life. I have always dreamed of him. I have always wanted him. I think I always will.

I cannot describe the eeriness of my mind's vision of this man. He is always there. I don't know who he is, but he is my benchmark for love.

Chapter 7

S adness overcomes me. Giant sobs of loneliness sting my racing heart. The faint sound of footsteps leaving as you walk out the door. Lingering scents of teardrops stain the bareness of my being. I drown in an ocean of letdown as I measure my distance to the end. The closing of my possible future approaches as my last gasps of breath are pulled from me. I lay motionless in the warm tears that melt off the coolness of my body. The stillness frightens me as I face my final fear. I am drowning in sorrow.

I briefly held what was not mine to continue.

Disappointment creeks up behind me as loudly as the eerie sound of an old cast door. Words sting like the lashing of icy leather on bare skin as I think of my frustrations with him.

Answered by the familiar sound of harsh voices gone astray I am left whimpering; Like a reprimanded puppy at the end of a Master's long day… Small and wounded, eyes sadly looking for the comfort of Love. Before long I am found, restless and humble. Something like the horizon of new day. Notes of sadness play in the background, resting gently on the wings of relationships' hope.

Moments like these invite thoughts of him; of his voice, of his touch, of his kiss. Aches of desire within me; lost amidst the memory of passion. His breath on my shoulders, the light, the fire, the intensity of his eyes gazing in my direction.

His soft, wet kisses on my what-seems-like everything-at-once, leaving tingles up my spine. The coldness of his tongue melting ice cubes on my skin. Taught muscles and forgotten sensitivities yearning for him. His touch, his kiss, his warmth. Missing moments of future hope. Waiting in the present.

Still I am waiting. Expecting what may never come. Setting up my heart for yet another self-willed letdown.

I am anxious. I want to know what is real. I find myself aching to find my truth. Surprisingly, the ache comes without pain. It simply comes like the ease of which I find the air for my next breath.

Yet through it all, through every unfulfilled dream, I gain strength, finding the will to push through to the love I crave and the passion I desire. The selfless, foolish, strength of emotion my soul endlessly searches for.

The same emotion I find myself questioning. Do you truly exist?

I wonder sometimes if I have ever known love, beyond the surface of initial butterflies and immediate comfort…Beyond the dream of tomorrow masking the reality of today. Have I ever reached into the heart of love, into the burning intensity of all I have ever dreamed of and risked the fiery burn that melts away all of my *learned* reason?

Have I ever had the chance and just never taken the risk? Am I able to risk it all on one unclear shot for the sake of my soul's desire for more? I found out that I am and it does not always end in my soul's desire. It sometimes ends in heartache.

My mind is whirling above the slowed beating of my heart. I am resting for a moment, hoping to see him. Are you my dream or are you my comfort? Perhaps you are both and I have been too blind to see. Perhaps you are neither and I am a fool for love.

A strange solitude echoes around me. An imagined comfort is now dull and rough like the burn of skin after the edge of razor. Red and tender, I wallow, while thoughts of you race in my mind.

Crazy thoughts gone astray now cause the bleeding of my heart. A collage of feelings begin tomorrow, made up of dark shades of today.

I sit here and I miss him.

There is a distant echo within me. Hours pass giving him strength inside me. I can feel him moving, attacking the harmony of my soul. He chips away at my once growing strength, leaving me bewildered. Confusion sets in and I am left lost. There are moments of softness. There are moments of solitude. There are moments of aching desire. Here I am, defenseless, being attacked by Loneliness.

The sadness that consumes me is not in the formal sense. There is no longer a driving of tears. There is no craved hunger or forced starvation. My nerves are intact. I am able, most times, to focus, though part of me is still longing, yearning, waiting. There is a growing anticipation within me to hear the sound of his voice; to be in his presence. This weight that pulls on my heart leaves me on edge and solemn. I am fighting missing him with the same strength I fought loving him. The emptiness that has formed is so much more than sadness, it is loneliness for unknown things.

I am frightened by the loss of Him. I am awaiting his call. I am in a hallway of darkness, hoping for light. Images of my past haunt me; teasing me with memories of brighter days.

I am lost tonight. I am awaiting some form of direction. I am in the densest of imaginations forest, surrounded by the hardness of green.

I am lonely tonight. I am awaiting his return. I am counting the seconds as they crawl by. Small and slow like snails they pass me, marking the coming of hour.

I am sad tonight. I am missing him. I am remembering his touch, his kiss, his smile. The intensity of comfortable moments linger, beckoning to me.

I am alone tonight. I am watching for him. Staring out into nights end, anticipating the sound of him.

I am. I simply am. A combination of feeling and wanting and dream. He is too. We are...and yet, mysteriously enough, not together.

The day has finally come to an end and evening threatens with dark clouds and lingering moisture in the air. It is like the dance of darkness. The combination of the hours.

I am weighed down by yesterday's disappointments that creep into today's seeming potential.

Disappointments that remind me of paths gone astray, of decisions gone sour, of choices that will soon bring me the unavoidable pain I knew would come.

And like the hardness of foundation my emotions are held, protecting the emptiness of impossible dreams. Dreams brought on by unwarranted hopes. Hopes stemming from a lifetime of clouded reason.

And like the wee hours of darkness hanging on the coming of sun I await you. The possibilities of a new day...

Here you are again, alone this time. A vision of hope, of love, of pain. A twist of fate, a crazy thought, an image of you, of me. You smile, you nod, as if my mind sends you messages of time. You stop, you glance, your hand touching mine. Your scent, your skin, your embrace. And then I am stirred. I wake and you are gone.

There are countless days in every hour that passes. I watch the clock in anticipation of a new moment. The future vague, yet colourful enough to keep my mind in captivation. An endless whirl of complicated thoughts haunt me, tease me, beckon to me. That voice which echoes throughout my life… a constant tremor of sound luring me in a new direction.

I look up. The world stops. This could be madness.

This could be sanity. This may be
an expanse of new horizons.

This could be my heart and my soul.

This is my destiny.

I searched forever, hoping I would find you.

You are perfect in my eyes.

In no way comparable in the least, to anyone
or anything I have ever known.

You lift my spirits and hold me down.

You keep me alive and crush me.

You are a paradox; my eternity and my salvation.

You are a fantasy and a reality.

My world revolves around you.

You enlighten me. You charm me.

You make me believe the impossible. My Dreams.

Chapter 8

What if everything we saw of each other, every personal scent, every story of moments that touched our lives, but didn't necessarily include us, were nothing more than layers of moments, masking the real softness of who we actually were? What if all this, all we experience every day, were a façade? A tiny white lie lost in a larger untruth.

If that was our life, how would any person say that they knew another? How could a person know another? What is it, to know?

And so my mind goes on, as it always does; questioning learned truths.

Some days, like today, I have random thoughts that pull me forward with gusto; forcing mind's expansion. It is on those days that I find myself in comfort, challenging the foundation of my existence. Contentment follows comfort. I have felt my softness.

Then, as if like clockwork, I am forced back to routine. Focused thoughts race out looking for a home. Never a moment's peace, yet my mind rests.

My mask is on and I am gone.

I walk slowly as I face the cold breeze and drizzling snow. My walk to the car seems longer now. The jacket I find myself wearing brings me no warmth. My hands cold and dry, my lips chapped, but I walk on. Just two more blocks to go.

The weather gets worse around this time every year. Only two more blocks to go. My mind wanders and my eyes fixate on a warm fire, a large bowl of steaming soup, and a glass of Whiskey on the rocks. My stomach warms at the thought. Whiskey always was my favourite. It has been a while, and I could always use a shot.

I can barely feel the cold anymore. My face and arms are numb now. I don't acknowledge the presence of anyone around me. Thousands of lives drifting as the snow does; soft and delicate, and in their own little spaces. In the end the flakes all pile up together. Kind of like people, if you think about it. We all end up on the other side eventually. With this weather, at least the dead have the benefit of heat.

One more block…Still fighting the snow. My knees stiff and my joints are grinding. The snow is packing tighter now. Just a little while longer. Shouldn't be too bad.

Finally the end of the street. No more walking. I have no jacket. No warm car awaits me. There is no Whiskey and there is no steaming soup. I do have one thing. I have the power to give up, right now, and join the flakes as they drift together. You will never forget me. I fought for life, I fought for strength, but I give up this time, for freedom.

Chapter 9

I am alone. I walk alone. I think alone. I eat alone. I sleep alone.

I am lonely. I am afraid. I was always afraid...Afraid of you. Afraid of me. Afraid of consequence... Consequences lead to closure. Closure marks the end.

Even in the end I am alone.

I know nothing. I walk through life seeing nothing, hearing nothing. I know no one. I do not exist.

I walk through the footsteps of a stranger to avoid living my own life. What is it exactly that is wrong with me? The smiles, the laughter, I have none of it. The shadows surrounding faces are darkened by the shadow of the moon. The twinkle of unknown eyes bewilder me at times. I am surrounded by objects of beauty, of life's marvelous excitements, yet I can't feel them. I walk on heated sand at night searching for life. I forget I am alone. I am conquering mystery. I am fighting the unknown. I have chosen my current destiny. I am choosing to walk alone.

What is it that we call life? Breathing and eating? Those are the essentials. Loving and feeling? Those are optional. Existence involves being. Being involves another.

I exist because I am. I am because you allow me to be. I live through you. You bring out my best emotions. My qualities shine through you. My existence depends on you. Without you there is nothing to prove I exist. There are records and documents of course, but who really cares to read those? And besides, how would I, out of millions, be known? Who would think to look for me?

Every life is lived through someone else. Memories, photos, pictures of a night on the town, are existence. Who are you? You are me, and I in turn are you. We exist within each other. Inevitably, we are both dead.

Life in fact, may be all that surrounds and touches us but does not necessarily include us. We are all that another being allows us to be.

I am important because you love me. I am spited because you hate me. I am only nothing when you have no emotion. I suppose even hate is better than non-existence.

Today's bitterness sends shivers to my bones, as masks of whiteness cover the freshness of spring. Vibrant petals of red dance against faint shadows of gray, hitting sight as paint hits canvas. The brush of life casting colour through the sky as dreams of tomorrow's sunrise shimmer. The brightness of what-may-be sun vibrates against the bleakness of this day. Warm rays cast down upon me leaving drops of saltiness on my face. Winter begins again with the shedding of frozen tears.

A blizzard of whiteness drowns me. A brisk cold wind takes my breath away. Silent moments of solitude as I find myself lost in pure, white magnificence. Confined by the restraints of season, I am left stranded. The harshness of reality sets in as I wonder if I will ever again see the warm light of your face shine upon me. Lost thoughts of emotion and confusion consume me, as my barren existence dawns upon me like the rising of the sun. Words float around my mind endlessly, falling into whatever space they may find. The poor visibility of this snow storm reflects the uneasiness of my mind.

Blessed by the purity of winter and held together by the coldness of season, shadows of doubt, hidden by the darkness of night, dance somberly until the coming of sun. The dance of freedom from distant rays of sadness dripping like icicles off festive sleighs, all being captured by the lens of the moon; shining dimly from behind masks of purple skies. Beyond the magic of this moment I stand, tall and black among images of whiteness.

I feel odd. My thoughts are odd. I am surrounded by oddness. The mediocrity of today leaves me overwhelmed. The cool breeze leaving me frozen beyond feeling. I am angry. I am frustrated. I am confused. I am constantly battling the paradox of me.

And yet here I am. Writing...

Like the rising of evenings star you reach me. Watching from afar... sending rays of promise in my direction, calling my name, taunting me from what seems like miles away. All the while, I feel you. Your presence lingering over moments of restlessness, sadness, discomfort, and love...

Endless moments of illuminated thought circle the uneasiness of my being... steering me off chosen paths gone astray, leading me in new directions of seeming happiness.

And in moments of happiness you are shaded. Masked behind the densest of storms' cloud; allowing me to grow, and learn, and feel. Sheltered and quiet, you are idled, unnoticed, unmissed...

Until the bitterness of winter's chill returns... Bare skin meeting the coldness of frost; freezing the very realness of Joys' warmth. The last of pleasure's energy spent searching; suddenly feeling the loss of your gaze.

Like the eternalness of parental love, you lift me; reminding me of happiness, sheltering me from the hardships of life. The tranquility of eternal grace is upon me once again, as I gently fall back into the steady arms of Hope.

Chapter 10

My life changes as I sit in silence. The softness of the cool breeze glides softly across my skin as I write. I find myself missing everything. I find myself missing you. It has been some time since I have written from my heart. I am alone, and what is worse is that I am lonely.

A grand sea harbors me. A sandy beach with crystal skies. The palm trees sway. The leaves shudder; cool breezes have begun.

Ice cream days and coffee nights. A time, a fill, a moment.

The water crashes, the clouds darken. The snow will begin again.

A voice echoes in my mind; A smile haunts my dreams. It is beautiful, it is lonely, it is longing. It is Distance.

Deep within my memories, I find the happiest and saddest of times. Living within my sheltered world, barely enough time to take note of the beauty that surrounded me; The innocent and genuine smiles, the plentiful laughter, or the rampant ways of the thunder.

Then with a sudden chill, winter comes, leaving me blinded and numb. Overcome by emotions, a sudden tragic loss from what seems like nowhere, like a snowball building in a child's hand. An immense form growing within me... The weight of pain.

And then, when I thought I could not go on, a sudden burst of joy.... Rebirth... a child is born and the seasons have changed.

Love is restored to a life of emptiness before I realize that I have only touched the surface of the immensities I may come to feel.

Here I am again, pensive this time, thinking back on my memories, reliving my pain....

Wondering what may have been, what might have happened. A delusional confusion... lost amidst the darkness.

Then a burst of light at the end of my tunnel; steering me, guiding me, luring me into yet another roller coaster of emotions. Afraid and unsure I follow you, wondering where this path may lead.... Hoping, wishing, wanting...

Do you know how I feel?

Chapter 11

Music plays endlessly as the ink stains my paper. What is it that I really want? I have filled my life with vast and empty nothings. Nothings have consumed me.

I am finally here wanting so much more. I have all of life's comforts and still feel as if I have nothing at all. When did more become so important and how long, I wonder, have I ignored it?

I write to you as a faceless image. A form I do not know and cannot see. I know there will be no response and perhaps that is why I reach out to you.

Here I am, trying to understand my being. What is it that preoccupies my thoughts?

Time slows as I sit and gaze. An eternity of *nevers* stare back at me. A life of love and fullness speaks, as though reading my heart and mind. All newness is restored, all power is regained. I see innocence. I see strength. I see you.

I am greeted with the warmth of the sun. Smiling, unknown faces surround me as I break to capture this moment. The beauty of this day overwhelms me leaving me in a state of emotion. My pen glides over the softness of this paper as thoughts race out to be recorded. The comfort of this newness reminds me of your shining face; the brightness of your eyes comparable to this magnificent sun. The warmth as incredible as your embrace.

I find myself missing you… your laugh, your voice, your magic. The same magic I feel now as I reflect on my days at home.

The magnificence of the sunshine; the magnificence of your being. The magical moments of my life.

Chapter 12

Vibrations from the hands of time cast shadows of memory across the tiles of my life. Innocence of youth now masked by the reality of adult existence. Small special moments in time engraved forever in a hiding place of Real. A real as rough and tender as the marking of new love on bare park trees. A forever-ness of warmth and smiles look on from distant lands of love and friendship. Lands of eternal confidence governing the splendor of Heroes.

The first man in my life… ensuring my survival, my safety, my home. My best friend. My confidante. The air I breathe at times.

The sounding board of my life. The miracle of my father.

When I think of my life, I think of you. Always standing tall above me; stern and strict, guiding, leading, and nurturing… Mom. Once upon a time such a distance… unable to speak, to talk, or to be. With a lack of emotion we trudged along, hoping to find a common ground. And here I am today… a vast part of me is you. You have had a hand in who I am, who I have become. You have given me strength to stand tall and strong. You have brought me through the hardest times, kept our family as one. You are more than my mother. You have become my friend. In becoming a mother I have learned to appreciate all that you are and all that you do.

What can one say about a sister? My confidante. The oldest child in our family; the benchmark for family standards. A shoulder to cry on in my weakest of hours. One look from you can break me, can drive me down emotions road to turmoil. You bring out the emotion in me, the love, the life.

In the wee hours of night or first thing in the morning we cross paths. We share laughs and jokes and fight over space and principle. You always were stubborn... Somehow, so was I.

Before long, we are adults; discussing life, and love, and possible future direction. A third party parent to look up to. The first child to know the alarm code. (I had to cry for mom to tell me). Did I mention I'm still annoyed about that? I swear I wouldn't have slipped.

When I think of the time we spend in life's depth or circumstance's nonsense, I smirk. You are my Beast (nickname). You are my Sister.

There are no words for my brothers. Mountains of emotion build up inside me. I cannot describe the intensity of love I feel for them. I watch them now, grown into fine young men. Both handsome and intelligent in their own unique ways. I look at my brothers, and envision my children. I admire them from afar, and push them forward to realize all that they are capable of becoming. My two angels right here on earth. You are friends, confidents, shelters from the worlds' chaos. You are much like my children sometimes... yet adult versions of. You melt me with one word. You are my life's combination of both strength and weakness... You evoke both. And now as adults, you support me. You help me. You console me. You are magnificent men.

I am home at last; Surrounded by the vibrant greenness under a pale blue sky. The soft hum of cool air taking me away to another place... Distant and tranquil, like the calmness of a Crystal lake. As I breathe in the familiarity of this moment I am elated. Thoughts race and memories flash. I am awakened by the freshness of your voice. Immersed in the beauty of today's crispness I wander, searching for the meaning of today. I have been captured by the splendor of Calm.

The distant sunrise casts shadows on an otherwise sunny day. The scent of sadness lingers heavily in the air as I anticipate the coming of a storm. The once gentle breeze wraps me in anguish as I melt into the trickling stream of emotion.

The vagueness of morning condemns me, as I stand alone on stage. Blinded by the spotlight of interrogation, I falter. I am circled by ravens of loneliness….My mind whirling with imminent thoughts of desire. An uncertain audience gazing in my direction.

I am unable to respond… searching for the strength to breathe. Just as I have chosen to give in, you appear before me in all your magnificence… sheltering me from the bright beam that examines the depth of my soul.

I am swept up in your softness… It is Comfort.

Chapter 13

*T*he brightness of your being overwhelms me. My thoughts whirl endlessly as if I am trapped in the gusto of storm. The magnificence of your features inviting crazy thoughts and impossible dreams. I am caught somewhere between the warmth of the rays and the brisk softness of the wind.

I look to the horizon. I see the sun. You are brilliant.

And like magic I fall into your gaze. I watch from afar and I am captivated by the greenness of your eyes. The gleaming brightness sounding out, summoning me to the feared warmth of your being. Your intensity drives me to a new direction, guiding me into a world of unstable grounds. I am blinded by your brightness, stumbling to find my way. I am reaching for you. Will I find your hand?

Soft scents of newness linger in the air as pastel shades consume quiet moments. Sparkling eyes and ice cold drinks mask the restoration of ancient times. Savory aromas surround endless chatter as souls wait in anticipation for the coming of destiny.

And so another day begins with a scent of uncertainty... misty skies begin to mask the brightness of the sun, and wetness hangs heavily in the air.... The long-ago-storm has parted but its presence is constant.

Chapter 14

Quite recently, someone very close to me chose against a major operation and opted for the borrowed-time option of existence.

What hurts me, and literally breaks my heart, is not even the idea that fear of pain, physical or otherwise, is more frightening than death, but that one could believe that they have no reason to live. The idea that one could feel that deep sense of loneliness practically brings me to tears.

One may argue that years of burned bridges, bad choices, and misguided routes could certainly lead one to the dead end of solitude, but with all of the kind hearted, loving, mistake-making individuals in this world, when did embracing another in their time of need become less of a priority?

I find myself saddened, beyond what I have felt in the longest of times. It is almost as if I am already experiencing the loss that has not yet come. In some ways, I know I may have contributed by not being enough, not showing enough, not spending enough time. There were countless days when the craziness of life seemed so overwhelming that I could not seem to find a moment to catch my breath or collect my thoughts. Off I ran, taking a long drive, finding a comfortable bench in the park, sitting, writing, being one with the world, all the while, neglecting those around me that I was too busy to be with. Those I neglected, as an aside, were generally those who have helped create the foundation of my life. They are the legs I stand on and the air I breathe at times.

I ask myself, am I truly sad about my loved ones' loneliness as the compassionate individual I am, or am I feeling guilty that I let time pass and now it has run out? Is it a combination of both? Is my sadness really some form of self-inflicted shame? Perhaps sadness is not an emotion at all. Perhaps sadness is a term given when one feels partially responsible for one component in the whole scope of a situation gone astray. Sadness is like no other emotion. It is triggered by loss or misfortune; a combination of mixed emotions, mostly ending in pain.

My first thought is to say that I am sad today. My second is that this reality check will probably knock me back on track and teach me a valuable lesson. Life is not as long as it should be or could be. There are good times and bad. Good choices and bad. Good people and bad. Regardless of the circumstances or what category you fit into, time is what it is... passing us by.

Chapter 15

I grew up with my brothers and sisters. There are four of us. One older sister and two younger brothers... Somewhere in the middle, I am. We grew up as normal siblings; fighting, playing, and sharing. We have a remarkable bond. A binding love and loyalty that holds us together in the most true and genuine measure of relationships bar.

There was a point in my life when I was too naive to understand that we had almost lost the youngest of our clan. A dreadful blood disease threatened his existence. He was cured and life was restored to normal. My parents ate dinner at home. My mom didn't sleep at the Hospital. We didn't have news reporters knocking on our door. We began to live like children again. Then we all grew up. It seemed that God wanted to test our strength of will because years later, it all happened again. This time, conscious awareness made moments of waiting much more difficult than they once were. I am frightened. I am terrified. I cannot fathom that there has been a time in my life when I thought I truly had a problem. Nothing, not one thing I have ever known or seen has brought me to this new level of low. I watched the dynamics of our family change. I watched as each of us faced our own fears. We watched the youngest of our siblings face his. Life became a blur for me. Inevitably, we all faced the same thought. What if, God forbid... I cannot bear to finish that thought. I am not strong enough. I am definitely not large enough.

There are times in life when we are in control of everything. There are times in life when we choose to be passive. There are times when life drives you to your knees, reminding you, that when it counts, you can and will be left defenseless.

When I think of those yesterdays, I feel emptiness. Vast tomorrow's and awry endings surround me. Wishes, wants, desires. Dreams of Domani's blessings. Forgotten goodbyes and tearful joys; instant thunder and sunny clouds. Awakened senses and lonely moments. One thousand four hundred and forty minutes of oggi. Will Domani ever come?

Through the ups and downs, the joys and sorrows, the tragedies and memories that we call life, lies our inner strength. On this, we depend.

I sometimes wonder what drives me to be all that I am. I live in a world of softness trapped in a larger void of emptiness. Days pass and I find myself confused. Not sure of who I am or my greater destined role. Is there one? I trap myself in walls of chaotic craziness. A world far removed from my own. I then seek out strength. Strength I feel I have yet to find. I am the centre of unhappiness. The role I have somehow come to know. I desperately scrape life's door, begging to be let in. Here is where I find myself. The me of who I am.

The smallest of life's events is paralyzing. We all face the same fears and the same thoughts of sadness bring each of us down with one gust of reality's breeze. The realness of moments passing reminds us of our own life desires. Desires we have long let go of. A path opens up before each of us. Somehow, even though enlightened, we are guarded.

Hidden strength reveals itself as the grace of Holy's light falls down on us. Truth battles fear in the war of worlds, showering us with moments of intense uncertainty.

Somewhere, far below, life goes on. Thousands of unaffected people living as they do. Laughing as they do. Somewhere not so high above, we are. Moments of longing mask another day of seeming emptiness. Gazes of love fight off moments of despair and paths too long become defined. Days of freedom entice you as the soul of Hope lives on.

Then a miracle, prayers were answered, and my brother is released home.

Chapter 16

*L*ife goes on. It goes on after birth. It goes on after death. It goes on after heartbreak and intense fear. *Or does it?* People say that life goes on, but my life, which has been affected in such a drastic way, doesn't just go on, it goes on differently.

Unless you are the Son of God, it is only reasonable that what you consider to be a life-moving, monumental event doesn't cause the earth to miss a revolution. No matter what happens to me during the entire sum of your existence, the sun always rises, the wind continues to blow, and those around you, those millions of beings that never come close to touching your life, never skip a beat. Routines don't change... *well, except for mine.*

In fact, my life is not "going on" the same way at all. I am living differently. I am sleeping less, eating more, working more, and wallowing in my self-pity. Apart from the essentials of a living, human being, breathing, eating, sleeping, my life is NOT going on at all. I am living a new life, learning a new routine, finding a new groove.

What resistance to change. What resistance to starting anew. Is it fear of another possible failure or success? Is it a bruised ego or a loss of comfort? Whatever it may be, my life is not my-life-as-I-know-it anymore. Times have changed. I may or may not have taken part in the decision, I may or may not have been the catalyst for the change, but in fact, my life is different.

So here I find myself, at whatever age I currently am, wondering how on earth I got here. I question my motives, my emotions, my principles, and maybe even, my existence. All the while, the ones I love most find it in their hearts to pass on the same words that they were once told. "Life goes on." And so it does.

The world is still turning. The people I have never come to know in my entire presence on earth still find it in their hearts to go to work, shop, eat, and buy new furniture, regardless of my newfound joy or sadness. Children are born, family members pass on, pains come and go and before long, it dawns on me. Life just keeps happening. It may not be my life, but life, nonetheless. I hate to be the bearer of bad news in this seemingly perfect world, no matter what anyone may tell me, my life will never be the same.

Chapter 17

*D*o all things end, I wonder? When I was twenty, my parent's relationship ended. Well, their relationship still exists, but on a somewhat different level. In many ways it is still the same.

I sometimes ask myself where people go wrong. There must be a build up of frustration, anxiety, boredom, and tension, but when is it, that one experiences that one brief moment where conscious mind marks the end? Is there a pause at this moment? Is there a brief reflection moment? Does it sweep over you like a revelation? Do you wake up after a long restful sleep and realize that your life is not what you want it to be?

All things end eventually. Lives End. Songs end. Days end. I should be used to endings by now. Somehow, they don't seem to be getting easier. As a matter of fact, they seem to get harder to get over. Endings don't just end like they once did. Now they take part of you with them. They take part of your faith, part of our hope, part of your self-confidence. The older and wiser you become, the easier it is for endings to bring you with them.

All things eventually begin again. They are always different. They are always new. They always lead to a new form of 'end.' Life is a series of pre-determined time allotments. It seems as if life is a CD that was left on repeat.

Love's ending carries so much heartache. For me, companionship's ending is most likely the worst part of it all and has always been the last and hardest part of the lost relationships' healing; the loneliness that follows the loss of a companion. The place you find yourself when everyone else is out with their respective loves, perspective loves, or families and you find yourself in the familiar spot of missing the one you love. The place where what you need, apart from time to lick your wounds and wallow in your self pity, is a new constant. Initially, a person who is there for the morning call, the afternoon call, the goodnight call, and the weekend activities. Someone to call when you just had a fabulous moment at work, or the worst meeting ever.

In times of relationships end, we all need a relationship fill in... Just long enough for the ego to forget that it has once again been bruised. For me, the relationship fill in is followed by needing something for me. Some return to myself to bring me a renewed happiness. Something to return me to the comfort of being just me.

First I experience the sadness and reality that comes from the immediate break of the routine that I've come to know and love. Then the loss of the intimacy and loving. Followed by the loss of all the things that touch the relationship. Friends, in some cases children, and the dynamic that came with them. Lastly the companionship. Somewhere mixed in there is the loss of the sense of belonging. And how wonderful it is to feel like you belong.

When do our lives stop meshing to mark relationship's end? Is there one common moment of enlightenment that we all feel? Do feelings ever really end, or do they just change form, shape, or intensity?

I wonder if my fear of endings restrains me from beginning again today. Perhaps I anticipate the end before I even begin. If that is the case, will destiny risk carrying me to where I am supposed to be?

Chapter 18

I wait in anticipation of your call. I yearn for the sound of your voice. Your being haunts my dreams. Dreams that I know may never become reality. I have created a world in you; A world of hopes, of dreams, and of unwarranted suspicions. It is in this haze that I seek you. I know fully that the world I have created is entirely my own. You do not see me, you do not accept me. You may not even love me.

Foolishly, I continue to wait as many did before me, long before my time. You are captivating my mind with your absence. You are unaware that you have created a void in me. An emptiness I once filled with hope. Hope that has gone astray.

Hope that I fear may never come. I wait in anticipation. I am hoping you will call.

When I think of losing faith, I often try to trace back to the initial bar or standard I have set for myself and for my life. I think of the marks I have placed on my history that have become the standards that govern my existence; the benchmarks that have created the standard that I live by.

I suppose this partners with my non-negotiables. There are some things in my life that I just can't live without. Some days it seems that everyone and everything are above the bar. Some days, every moment seems disappointing.

I remember once, many years ago, when my father was let down by one of his closest colleagues. He sat in his black leather chair, reclined, hands behind his head, lying there emotionless. Not a line of expression on his face. I asked him what was wrong.

He replied, "I've lost faith in humanity." Those words and his expression will be etched in my mind forever.

I vowed to never let anyone bruise me to the point of saying those words, for the rest of my life. That was then. I was young then.

Here I am now, at whatever age I am, half-heartingly believing in emotions, humanity, and existence.

I have had many blessings in my life. I have been surrounded in comfort. I have never wanted, in the formal sense of the word. Never did I pray or have to plead for the necessities of life. I have lived a comfortable life. I was afforded many luxuries growing up in my family. I was surrounded with greatness. I was surrounded by great and intelligent people. I still am.

The bar of my life, my standard for existence, was founded in part, by my lifestyle and upbringing, and those who took a part in shaping who I am today. The strength of these great faces set the first standard of existence for my life. They taught me what to expect, what to reject, what to be leery of. Then I grew up. I am adult. I am educated… both academically and independently. I have filled my mind with many thoughts, some others, some my own. Each sentence I have read in the course of my existence, partially dissected, broken down, and stored somewhere in the engine of my mind. The gears turn and a new standard is born. This one entirely my own.

Life's beauty and bleakness impose themselves on me. The imposition of life; what an incredible concept brought to my attention by an incredible man. Here these impositions find me. Some wonderful. Some painful. As I process my emotions I wonder which bar, which standard of my existence is using its fury to mark the perspective on my thoughts. Is this the standard of my foundation, or is this my own? Did they mesh somewhere along the way when I wasn't taking the time to notice?

My unique measure of success that has brought me to my own seeming greatness has also led me to a path of great disappointments. I have my very own double-edged sword...

I often wonder where my standards end and I begin. Did I really lose faith in humanity or have I lost faith in myself?

When I think of what governs my existence I am in limbo. My childhood conditioning or my adult experiences. When disaster strikes, which impulse will I follow? If my foundational standard weighs heavier than my own, whose life am I really living? If not my own, who am I?

Chapter 19

*H*onesty fascinates me most. What exactly is honesty? I honestly like you. I honestly tried my best. I honestly didn't mean to. How many people can actually 'take' another honest individual?

One can banter back and forth about truth; what it is in theory, in practicality, what it is period but truth is in part fictional; A belief like any other. The truth: Sometimes what you want to believe, sometimes what someone else wants you to believe; sometimes what you want others to believe. Truth may have very little to do with fact.

Being honest is essential to human peace of mind. People feel better knowing they are not being lied to. What happens, then, to this desire for honesty, when the honest 'truth' is hurtful, or worse than that, something you don't want to hear? What if the honest 'truth' is something you weren't prepared to hear?

Battle gear goes on. Vicious words are used as weapons, all the while, at least one of the two parties, *one would hope*, feels terribly that being 'honest' about their feelings has led their partner to pain.

The inevitable battle will follow, as your 'honest' gut feeling foretold. Hurt feelings want revenge and add insult to injury. Pain enters the argument, bringing with him, tears and awkwardness, and maybe even regret. At least one of the two parties realizes they have gone too far, but still the battle continues. Ego finds his home... Onward we go until energies are exhausted and the battle ends.

Fatigued minds and bruised souls return to the place they know best... their place. The place within where no one has ever been. The place one goes for refuge. Still the mind reels with the 'honest' and 'truthful' perspective they have just gained on their relationship.

Time goes forward, as it always does. The earth still hasn't missed a revolution for you, not even in your time of relationship strain. Your partner, at some point, returns, somewhat normal, perhaps a little more guarded. You go back, less involved, more cautious, full of hurt. Eventually old wounds are healed. *Until the next time you decide to be honest about how you feel.*

Being honest and truthful about your perspective about life, and love, and partnerships, and your partner for that matter, doesn't give your partner happiness. It brings YOU happiness. It makes 'YOU' happy that you can be 'honest.' It makes you feel 'good' inside. It relieves something off your chest. One less thing to carry around, one less perceived truth... Even if the 'truth' you see is completely out of the realm of actual fact. Realistically, if you believe something to be true, can anyone convince you differently?

I can accept that being honest and truthful about what I believe may hurt some of the people that I love. There will be a day when I may be called selfish, or inconsiderate, or insensitive. (That may have been today) Perhaps I will at some point, lose the respect of someone I love. I think I can handle that. (Fast forward ten years and it turns out I can't) All that I am is encompassed in what I believe.

Perhaps all emotions are selfish in nature. Do we love solely in order to receive love? We avoid hurt to avoid inevitable pain. We are honest, to avoid accusation. Can it be possible that even with emotions there is always a hope of return?

I have often written of relationships hope. What is it that I hope for? Is it the anticipated call, the familiar sound of comforts voice, or the reintroduction of expectations and routine?

I am in seeming love yet again. This time all alone. He exists of course, the man I have my sights on. He is much larger than me. He is tall, guarded, and full of mystique. Naturally, his non-responsive nature has intrigued me. Glutton for punishment, who?

I am imagining that he doesn't know how I feel. I haven't told him. I don't think I will. I am working against the voice of reason in my mind.

I have nothing to lose, yet fear restrains me with all of its grandeur.

So here I find myself, an adult, daydreaming of not-so-real love. I see myself holding him, sharing with him, loving him. All of this existing in my very own world… my mind. Considering he isn't formally participating, apart from in my thoughts, things are going fairly well.

How many others before me have wasted countless days and hours imagining possible loves and opportunities?

How many others are afraid to face certain emotions head-on? Normally, I would exhaust every effort to show him, but today, I have decided not to.

I wonder how much of my imagined world is really what I actually want. Do I look forward to any of those moments or do they exist only in my imagination because they cause me so much fear?

If I could let my guard down, say my piece, and then disappear before responses fury, would I speak freely?

I have never been afraid and I have always been afraid. Fear of failure. Fear of rejection. Fear of loss. On the flipside, fear of conquering desire, fear of success, and fear of winning.

When all fear melts away, and all is as it rightfully should be, what comes next?

Chapter 20

I find myself thinking about the *meaning* of life… contemplating the importance of family and love and companionship. I am an adult. Somehow, *the rest of my life* has crept up on me. I am sitting here, on my laptop, writing this… I feel like I am outside the boundaries of life looking down at myself, wondering how I arrived where I am so FAST. When did I really become the me of who I am today?

Within the next five years, I will most likely be married. My friends have already made the jump… if not on their way to leaping as I write this. I think of myself and wonder, "Will I ever be ready?" I am an adult who is afraid to enter into the institution of marriage. The 'status' of being a wife, in any sense of the word, frightens me. For years, I have been bombarded with divorce statistics… and here I am, using this crutch as a declaration of 'commitment-phobia.'

Back to my future… *literally*. I will most likely get married. I eventually will be married. I want a family and I LOVE children. I definitely want to be a mother. I think I would rather be a mother than a wife. That was a hard statement… if I intend on 'keeping' my future beau, I shouldn't say things like that too loud, *let alone write them*. The truth is, for me, anyway, is that it is much scarier, to be a wife, than to be a mother. I remember hearing a woman I once worked with say, "When you become a mother, you sign up to be a doctor, lawyer, chef, taxi, teacher...etc, etc, etc." She was absolutely right. That is what my mom is.

What does it mean to be a wife? Before I answer that, I will give you some background. I have been working full time for many years now. I moved out of my family home at twenty-one. I enjoy working with different non-profit organizations and enjoy being involved in fundraising and fundraising events. I love to read, love to play, and absolutely love music and theatre. My mother and father are separated. They have been for many years now. My mother and father had a fantastic relationship. They have a fantastic relationship. I kid you not. My father helped clean up the table, they talked on the couch for hours every night, and my mom made sure my father was never late... a seemingly perfect relationship. Fabulous parents too. My mom was the disciplinary parent, my father, the beam of shining hope. The eternal 'good guy,' as my siblings and I often called him. Together: A Dream Team. My mother chased us with the wooden spoon when we were bad. My dad held the flashlight. Even when the power went out it was possible to get "the spoon."

When I think of marriage, I choke up inside. I wonder what it takes to be the perfect wife. Part of me listing the duties and routines that should be checked off while the rest of me believing fully in the power of love. I cannot imagine the hurt that follows 'losing' ones chosen life partner. I cannot imagine being another statistic. Looking back at my life, there were many times I could have been more supportive with the men I dated. I could have loved more, been more, done more. I cannot change those days.

Thinking about the stages of my life, I may be entirely wrong. Maybe marriage and future isn't the scariest after all. Maybe it is scarier to be a child. The unattainable expectations of your friends and family, the fear of letting your parents down, the most terrifying of all, the pressure of growing up. Maybe now that I am here, right where I am supposed to be, is where, with a clear scope, I may find the least scary part of my life. I have completed infancy, childhood, adolescence, and am an adult. The only thing left is my future.

Clouds of sheltered blush burst in the skies above, showering the world with pink ribbons and colourful bows. A commotion of chatter masked by the innocence of young eyes looking on…*a daughter is born.* Beaming faces radiating the hopes and dreams of a child's glory as visions of ballroom gowns and ballerina shoes complete the moment.

Long before a daughter understands *the process that accompanies family,* stem the dreams of her perfect days. Baptism, Communion, Confirmation, Marriage, not once forgetting her Graduation, Prom, first love, and first job.

Without realizing it, you are living another's dream. You find yourself travelling a predetermined path of happiness and success. Somewhere along the way, the *REAL* you, emerges. Who you are and what you have come to believe and accept, conditions the road you are travelling, making it just a little more *your path,* than it has ever been before.

Still there are the shared dreams of the perfect mate, the perfect life, and that ONE perfect day. *The fantasy of your wedding…*

Parents seem to have the most incredible expectations about the man their daughter will marry. They can't help but *rub off* on you. You want the ideal man… smart, honest, hardworking, and attractive. He should be kind and loving and family oriented. Naturally, you will be THE most important person in his life and he will court you and make you FEEL like a lady.

All the while, society is saying, "You have to be happy yourself before you can be happy with another," "You survived before him, you'll survive after him," and how can we forget, "You don't need a man to find happiness." *Life has changed.* There is no mutual need for a partner; one can make it on their own… *Even* a daughter.

What hasn't changed, over the years, is the mutual desire for the comfort of family, and love, and the comforts of home. The "need" for a partner may have been lost over the last decade or so, but if one had a choice between "needing" a partner and "wanting" a partner, wouldn't one naturally want the latter? There is a security that comes from knowing that your partner is *choosing to be with you.* Every day, for what you hope will be an eternity.

Armed with the above, a daughter is ready to tackle the world. She has standards, morals, and education. Off she goes to enter the whirlwind world of dating. Dating can really be stressful. The first heartbreak practically kills her. Second love, *a little more cautious this time around...* then a series of miscellaneous excursions, all leading up to the one that you love, *hopefully as you've never loved before.*

The One. I imagine that much to your surprise, he has the ability to aggravate you. You have to put in effort to make the relationship work. He wants a family, but he still wants to golf every Sunday. Dinnertime is 6:30 pm but he can't boil a pot of water. You have to teach him the ropes of "not living with mom anymore" and invest time in helping to make it work. Then it dawns on you... he has shit to teach you too.

There is no perfect life, no perfect partner, and no perfect day. There is only what you will put up with, what you will do, and what you will not do to make your life what it will be...*perfect for you.*

And just like that it happens... I grew up and the future has arrived.

I am destined to be here.
Destined to write this.
A letter from my heart to yours.
I am where I belong.
I am alone with my eccentric self.
Following the path laid out in front of me.
Knowing that some time, somewhere along the way,
I will find him.
My partner in every way. The one I am destined to be with.
Fate will follow me
Dressed as my knight in shining armour
Brightening my path, and
Filling it, even briefly,
With comfort.

Chapter 21

I sometimes wonder what it is that I really want. I wonder if all that I am, all that encompasses my being is enough, or if it is much too much for anyone to sustain. I have been drained in many areas of my life. I find myself pulled in many directions. I feel distant and detached, so far from my once chosen path. Am I growing up, or growing apart from all that holds meaning in my life? Perhaps one is meant to step away from foundation in order to expand. I always wrote about loneliness, isolation, and solitude. Perhaps I counterbalance it with a full existence of people and motion. I am fighting to express myself, always staged in front of a seemingly uncertain audience. How could one consistently feel alone? Why do I always find my soul is searching for more? What is it that my soul requires to satisfy its longing? Is it healthy to have an insatiable desire for more? Would a doctor prescribe a human with insatiable hunger a clean bill of health?

I am compensating for a void in my life. If only I understood what void I was trying to fill. What amount of soul searching will bring me peace of mind?

I always find myself here; licking my wounds in solitude with paper and pen, being comforted by melodies harmonic rhythm. The music changes. Even the pen changes. What doesn't change is the pattern of loneliness.

Why is my character so deep? Why are there so many spots in my being that are raw and tender to the touch? How many false layers of existence mask my heartache?

How can a heart so full of love to give feel so empty and alone?

I am lost in a world of emotion. There is no logic, or reason, or peace of mind. I feel distraught and bruised. I search for meaning I cannot find.

I feel closed in and sheltered from all that I love and all that brings me joy. I ache as I witness myself letting go of what I love.

I cannot find the catalyst for my confusion; confusion that marks the endless anxiety of my existence. I have lost myself. I feel mechanical.

I sometimes wonder who I am.

What I want to hear. What you want to be told.
A jumbled confusion; a murmur; a thought...
Mumbles under your breath, in anger, joy, or sadness.
Sometimes confusing and always debatable.
Sometimes constant and rarely consistent.
Sometimes furry or bright and yet mean and gloomy.
So many possibilities for you...
Some are said strong, and some are behind a mask of tears.
Some lead to smiles, while others lead to frowns.
So much a part of my life, an essential part of my existence.
A need and definitely a means of survival.
A source of description between one or more minds...
Words.

Chapter 22

*L*ike a newborn child with a lifetime of opportunity, this page lies. Screaming out to the nearest onlooker… begging to be charmed… and like the softness of breeze on skin, my words drape it. Swirls of ideas falling comfortably on imaginary lines of document conduct. Filled with rows of scattered thought and restless ideas…. The winding down of day…

Like the magnificence of morning's sun, this blank page excites me, as new thoughts race out to be recorded; anxiously waiting the judgement of mind. Here is where I find myself, writing to you, reaching out to be heard.

It was only very recently that the truth of timed existence had dawned on me. I woke up one morning to realize that I had completed another chapter of my life. My role as a student now part of my long ago past and I excitedly took on my future. It was not long after that I realized that real life had begun.

I have bills to pay. I have obligations. I am accountable to myself. Poor choices reflect on my ability as an adult to make a proper decision. A life full of responsibility has set in.

The whole process of growing up is over. I am here now, at whatever age I am, and while I will never stop growing as a person, *or growing older for that matter*, I can never not be an *adult* again. Like a ray of light after a night of darkness I am enlightened. I find myself seeing my family more clearly.

A new form of respect for my parents, *who once seemed so tall,* consumes me.... Reminding me how truly lucky I have been. I am amazed to find out that my parents, the two people who had instilled a seeming fear in me for what seemed like an eternity, are real people. As an aside, they are not so scary after all.

I find myself wondering how I could have missed the fact that my parents are normal people. They have their own issues, and problems, and idiosyncrasies. Here I am today, the apple that fell just far enough from the tree...Far enough to be able to grow and develop and exist as my own free spirit. Never once being held down or *shaded.* I thank you mom and dad, for that.

Part of my life has been scripted on a blank page of existence. A lifetime of memories scribbled in black and white while a future of possibilities are waiting to be realized. I will always be here, recording the story of me... one page in the story of 'man.'

Chapter 23

*D*o you see a star? Bright eyes, bright smile, clouded emotions on an otherwise sunny day. A multitude of unknown places waiting to be observed.

Fear casts chains on a free soul as soft, tense gazes fire across the room.

Somewhere along the way, seemingly destined souls have been conquered by doubts overwhelming strength; Strength that has kept possibilities at bay. Distance stands between us, marking the hardships of days to follow.

Misguided minds search out their fill, waiting for the moment of ever-sought after satisfaction. Somehow, in these moments of distance, destined souls part, leaving in their trail, a dusting of emotion.

Emotion that kindles when reunited, only to part ways once again.

The love shared between two hearts is far greater than the culmination of desire. Companionship guides us and we are calm.

Acceptance finds its home in our hearts and distanced souls find comfort.

Chapter 24

Friendships have come and gone and changed in my life. My world is a constant whirlwind of new faces, old faces, and dabbling participants.

I have friends that have left this world; friends I never had the opportunity to say goodbye to. These friends are etched in my soul for eternity.

I used to trust all of my friends. Then, I trusted some of my friends. Now I trust myself.

What exactly is a friend? Can any relationship stand the test of time?

Life is full of people who touch our lives but are never meant to be constants. Those friends I never expected would be there for me are always available when I need them most. The friends I thought would never let me down, were rarely there when my world seemingly came crashing down.

In my life, there have been those few, wonderful souls, that will always be the benchmark of what I consider to be, the best people I have ever known.

It is so beautiful here. The sun is shining so brightly upon the greenness of the world below it. Perfect music blends with the constant chirping of distant birds.

The breeze is cool and soft today. It shakes the fluttering leaves as it soars to find its way home. Soon you may leave too in search of your home.

A small trip that will begin the sadness that leads up to your eventual departure; A sadness I am not prepared to face.

And when I think of you, I think of all that I have become in your presence; All that I have come to know and feel. It reminds me of all that I will miss.

A constant, special, vibrant light in my life now threatens to turn a new direction

Fear consumes me. I may find myself without a guiding light.

Times change, decisions are made. Bena stays.

Then a man whom I respect and confide in meets the woman he has long sought after. Times change again, and a wonderful relationship flourishes. The kind we all hope and dream to find in our short time on earth.

Looking at a union of love inspires humanity… filling us with unique gusto, allowing us to radiate forward, positive wishes for the couple in love; Wishes of everlasting happiness; wishes of the meeting of each other's desires. It is with my entire heart that I wish every happiness to my best friend, and his destined love.

Chapter 25

I have wanted many things in my life. I have wanted to be close to many people.

Each time I faced desire, it was conquered by duties' call; A call to be honourable; A call to be loyal. Timing really IS everything...

There are days when I believe I have all that I could ever want. There are days when I am distracted by life's many temptations.

Each time I am tempted, I rely on the values instilled in me from infancy. I remember that betrayal is the worst suffering of heart and mind. It is not finite like loss of love, or loss of loved ones. It is eternal... a constant state of 'not good enough.'

Of course there is respect. Respect of oneself and respect of loved ones. Each day of companionship demands a new level of respect and dedication.

Each level of partnership requires honesty and integrity. Most important of all is loyalty.

I am loyal to my partner. I am loyal for him and I am loyal for me. I am not without weakness, but I can exercise constraint. Some days are harder than others.

I always remind myself of the moments I share with the man I love. Is anything worth the gamble of losing him? Is anything worth hurting him? I am quite positive there is not. Nothing would be worth hurting him. Nothing would be worth looking into his eyes and seeing anything other than love.

Just like that it happens. Feelings grow and commitment forms.

I am committed in heart and mind and body. I am not always committed in mind. Human nature leads you to wonder. What if, what if, what if...

I have no regrets. I have chosen wisely all along; wisely for me and wisely for him. I am committed to the man I love.

It has begun. Just like that it happens. Relationships form and lifetime partnerships unfold.

There are days when I am frightened. Is this all that I am? Is this all I will be? Is this all that I will pursue? Is this the beginning or is this the end? Perhaps it is the culmination of both. The end of one life and the start of new. The end of courtship and the coming of eternal comfort.

Each time I have doubt I remind myself that these doubts are the beginning; the beginning of the end. Doubt is followed by test of will. Test of will is followed by strength of character or disappointment of oneself.

Here we are at the end; the end of doubt or the end of seeming love. After the ending of doubt and seeming, all things are real.

Chapter 26

nother day begins. I can never understand the highs and lows of emotion's life. Why am I so sensitive today? Why does everything weigh so heavily today? Why do all problems seem heavier than usual? What makes the day, which I think of as today, one that is unbearable to me?

Why is today a day when I feel weak?

Why is my sentiment so outward? Between yesterday's normal, constant behavior, and this morning's waking up, was only last night's sleep. What about the hours of what-I-thought-to-be-peaceful slumber, was not?

Did I have nightmares? Am I still asleep?

Whatever happened between 1 am and 6 am has thrown off the following 10 hours of normal happiness.

I wonder if my mind has a preset timer of when to recycle and re-lay to rest, all the old dealt with heartaches and issues of the past, in order to make room for the newer, more recent memories of current life.

I am definitely not asleep but I wonder if I am awake.

Each day I leave the house in a mad dash to get to work, only to begin a full day of exhausting active management. From even before I wake, whirls of thought float around in my mind in anticipation of a new day.

Each moment skips by to the next, tasks are completed one at a time, and new tasks cycle down from a never-ending silo of duties.

The day ends and I leave the office in a mad dash to live before all energy has exhausted itself, leading me to another night of semi-peaceful slumber.

I pull into my driveway, the key opens the door, and I feel the great exhale of workdays end.

What madness is associated with responsibility. Yet here we are, striving to set new records, new levels, new targets; all an attempt to satisfy another day of 'living's' desires. Like a caged animal, I set out... new shoes, new pants, and new car.

An endless cycle of new that demands over half of my awake time.

Will there ever be a last new? I imagine not.

Chapter 27

My first love looked at me with intensity. His eyes burned into me. No one has ever looked at me the way he did. His look encompassed me; like the air within the bubble floating off the stick held in child's hand.

My first love gave me comfort. We had newness. We had purity. We had fights. We shared many moments and we shared our families. I loved sharing our families.

My love held me the first time I wanted to be held.

Our love was not tarnished by previous romance's heartache.

I will always love him. He was the first benchmark of relationships standard.

There were times in my dating life when I thought my boyfriend looked at me with that long ago glare that once made my heart race. It was like seeing a ghost.

First loves serve an important purpose in life. They are the first measure of the future love that you will come to expect...

The heartache from the loss of your first love humbles you after time's build up of confidences. My first love was special to me. He still is. When I think of his family, I think of my family. They are part of me. Burned on my soul. They have shaped in part who I am today.

Times change. Circumstances change. People change.

Feelings stay the same. Just like man, feelings adapt to their surroundings.

Here I am, at whatever point I am at, at whatever age I am, writing. I am older now. Needs change. Desires change. Life changes and will change again. I have found the love I was looking for. This is the last time I will love. Not in the formal sense of well-being, but the last time I will fall in love.

I have met the man of my dreams. I will write about him.

The first time I saw him I knew. From the moment we met, there was excitement and fear… the combination of passions.

There were times when I looked for something that didn't fit the logical, structured, order of my existence. Somehow though, he just fit.

From the day I met him, I have been afraid of life without him. I am alive again; after all the heartache, after all the fear.

Love walked into my life. Just like that it happened. I am in love.

I am lost in the sound of breeze.
Soft and constant and chilling to my soul.
Like a floating cloud I am drifting.
Being carried into a whirlwind of splendor.
A splendor unlike any I have known.
And like the weight of coming rain I am falling.
Being pulled into the realness of the world.
A world of loudness and peace.
A magical place I now call home.
A home that invites closeness
A gentleness that follows the dampness of storm.
The calmness of these moments overwhelm me
As I drift into the arms of you.

Chapter 28

*A*s he sits across from me, I see all that he is. I see his bright eyes and his boyish smile. I hear his soft voice as he sounds out confident convictions about life. There is a moment each time I am with him when all sound melts away. I watch his motions as he carries on, unaware of my defined focus. When he stops for a moment and I see him catch the softness in my gaze, our eyes part in a moment of shyness. It is in these moments that I am swept up in the comfort I feel in his presence.

My conscious mind reminds me that I have felt similar feelings before; though never quite like this and never quite so soon. Something magical is above us, showering us with a rare form of very new and very sure emotion. Emotion that seems to enlighten me... raising me up, restoring my hope in love.

My mind reminds me that I have yet to know him; yet to kiss him; yet to feel him. I have just begun to scratch the surface of the depth of this man.

Yet here I find myself, at whatever age I am, at whatever point I am currently at, completely intrigued beyond anything I have ever known.

Could it be that this is the feeling one associates with "the one?" Could it be that soul mates really do exist? Can soulmates really find each other in a seemingly chaotic world?

What is it, if not destiny, that has drawn me to this point? (I wrote this line on a piece of paper the first time I brought a coffee to the man who would be my future and likely only, husband)

And so I go on, as others have before me... finding a seemingly perfect love and slowly raising my guard.

My mask stays off, but the walls of fear begin to arm themselves, awaiting the signal that I may require shelter. It is with every effort that I fight them... *how exhausting.*

When I hear the softness of his voice my heart races. I wake in the morning in anticipation of our first exchange. What relief comes with our first connection... Oddly, I feel no sense of insecurity. There is no feeling of panic...I know somehow, that the much awaited phone call, will eventually come. *I am sure of it.*

I feel no strain or agitation. I am completely and blissfully content in the realness of this man's soul.

Fear lingers in the back of my thoughts... Fear of another heartache, fear of inadequacy, fear of once again, believing blindly, and fooling even the most inquisitive of minds... my own. I cannot forget the disappointment that follows relationships end.

Here I find myself. Transparent is what I am. (*Thank you RS for that*) There will be no more games, no more stolen, wasted, moments of time. No more 'learning experiences' that involve hidden feelings and words unsaid. There will be no more loneliness in my companionships. I have grown beyond this.

I have no fear of transparency with this man as my audience. I want him to see me. I want him close to me. I am confident that he has already accepted me.

What is it then that I am feeling, if not the beginnings of love?

Quite often we hear those three little words, "I Love You" prematurely and question what it is that our partner actually loves.

We have all been there. Two months in, gazing at each other across the table, holding hands; full bodied red wine has left our cheeks rosy, our inhibitions behind. Out flow the magical words that give us a false perception of comfort and trust.

What is it, I wonder, that we feel that can only be expressed with these vows of endearment? I love you should be a pledge of some sort, shouldn't it? When is it really love? Is it lust? Is it hope?

Perhaps at that very moment, gazing into new love's eyes, we find ourselves in a state of heightened emotions and forget that love, like trust, is earned, and grows over time. We forget that it takes years of support, emotional investment, sacrifice, and companionship, to really know love in its truest form.

Yet in these moments of intrigue, love is the only associated emotion of the heart and mind.

Then my phone rings and it is him. I am swept up again. The gentle sound of his laughter traces my skin and sets my mind racing. Hopefully an indication of what tenderness will come.

This may be the beginnings of love. This may not be the beginnings of love. This may be the entranceway into heartache.

This may be a series of passing moments sent from above, reminding me to never give up; to never settle. This could be my very own romantic miracle.

Having said all this, every day as I wake, his smile enters my mind like the flicker of spark off lighter's flame, and I feel for him, the most I can… he exhausts the full capacity of my available emotions.

I could be wrong about him (fear). I could be right about him (optimism).

Then again, this could be the very first time I have been fully present as love and comfort collide.

And then we meet again. His soft smile and gentle eyes entice me. Feelings of emotional desire growing within me…longing for the first feel of his, what I imagine will be, incredible touch.

He carries with him such confidence, yet child-like in moments of relationships words. The conversation of souls melts him, from what seems like the inside out.

Even in these times of shrinking back, he comes forward with an enticing grandeur. His passive and strategic approach is a perfect mixture of cat and mouse.

Just when I think I see him, a new level unfolds. He is marvelous in each layer, luring me with an insatiable desire for more.

When I feel the softness of his lips meet mine, I am ignited. A deep fire burns within me, desperately sending signals to be released.

Rational mind knows that passion will follow... slowly and softly at first and then strong, unreigned, and full of hunger. When I see him, I feel that hunger that I know burns entirely for him. It is almost as if it has always been there... *waiting*.

It is with much strength that I pull back. I am aware that it is much too soon for the conquering of desire. Time constraints that once caused frustration, so long ago, now carry with them thoughts of future ecstasy and splendor.

Then I look into his eyes and he fits. Just like that it happens. My heart and mind in synchronized thoughts for the first time since I thought I knew love.

What moments will follow this man, I am unaware. What path I will find myself encountering, I do not know, but intrigue has captured me, and I have no fear.

My new and transparent existence crashes with seeming perfection, giving birth to new dreams of futures that no longer seem so far away. Distant futures, but much closer to heart's eyes...

I find myself entirely captivated with what could be the shadow, or the substance, of a perfect love.

For the first time I was held in his arms. I found myself wrapped up in his incredible warmth... a warmth I had forgot existed, or never came to know. Every part of my skin ached to touch him, ached for some connection beyond our clothed embrace... Tingling with the not-so-often found strength of desire.

If you can picture this for a moment, I am lying in his embrace, completely content and wanting more… Frustrations building up inside me, begging to be released.

Yet here we find ourselves, caught in guarded walls of skin holding back in fear and anticipation.

I wake the following day yearning for the sound of his voice and the softness of his yet to be realized touch.

Everything about this man drives me, and in combination with the newness of it all, our relationships youth, I am left both anxious and elated.

The morning comes again, as it always does. Sometimes I see his name waiting for me on my screen, sometimes the phone rings and I am once again balanced.

This craziness I find myself wrapped in, completely enticing and captivating beyond reason. His responsiveness a sure sign of wonder yet to come; wonder I hope will find me at the most intense and perfect of moments.

I leave my daily routine to begin each evening's events. Part of me longing to be with him, part of me wanting to step back… Can too much time spent together damage a potentially perfect union? When two destined souls meet, can one action or inaction truly have a contrary impact? Somehow I am not overly concerned. Nothing indicates that this man will leave my side. Nothing indicates he is irrational or inexplicable. The only thing incomprehensible would be that of my intense emotions.

I believe I am falling in love. This time, I don't think it is seeming.

And so love enters my life again… this time less rushed… this time emotionally bonded… this time soulful…

As he holds me close to him in dance's fiery embrace, I am overwhelmed. My body and mind reeling with the intensity of being close to him. His scent lingers and I am drawn to kiss him.

His softness entices me… his softness drives me… into what seems like madness.

I cannot stop thinking of him. I cannot stop yearning for him.

He is so much more than I ever thought existed. I wonder sometimes if I am in a dream, meeting the love I have always searched for. Can this be real?

Can love come so soon? Am I being taunted by relationships hope? It cannot be…

This man is everything I have ever wanted in my life. I melt when I look into his eyes. I melt when I see his smile.

I will collapse into the first of his touches. My mind is a non-stop carousel of emotion.

And when I think of him, I smile. When I hear his voice, I am awakened.

I am in something every time I see him; and then again; and then again.

The notes play on and I caress his neck… dancing in what feels like an empty room… and then I am reminded there are onlookers and the momentary fire silences, only to begin again.

Not so much later, we find ourselves wrapped in desire's fiery embrace. Lips melt into each other and I am reborn. I am wrapped in the slender shape of his form, yearning to unleash the passion that has been building up inside me. As I sink further into the warmth of him, I feel his body press up beside mine… all of him… I feel the hardness of his form. I desire him.

Heated moments of passion spark like old wood in fireplace's home, crackling with excitement, and cooled by the coming of sun.

Then I am home, recounting moments I have shared with him, aching to have him near me, awaiting the sound of his voice…

Will I receive the evening's call I wonder? I can only hope…

How could it be that just when I thought he didn't exist, I found him? So often, rational mind conquers hope, leaving one whimpering with thoughts of disappointment.

One instant, one meeting, one kiss, can restore all hope in love; all hope in destiny.

I have met my match and I am elated.

It is Christmas time again. The snow is falling, decorated trees are sparkling, and families are celebrating. People are toasting health and happiness, and recounting the joys and sorrows of the months that have passed, beginning the countdown to a new year of possible outcomes.

I think of loved ones and relationships held dear. I plan for the future I hope will come.

This time of year is filled with so much reflection and love... it is a time of sharing and companionship, a time of renewed hope and brand new dreams... all of the things he represents to me.

The holidays race by with counted moments of intrigue. I am guarded but freer than I've ever been. I have seen a glimpse of shimmering love, similar to the promise of ceremonies diamond.

There is magic in this holiday season. Sprinkles of fairy dust land on our union, and how wonderful it is.

I lie in his arms looking into his eyes, imagining the ecstasy following his touch. And then in an instant, I can feel him. His body wrapped around me, draining me of brimmed desire again and again.

Every moment following, I ache for him... his touch, his scent, his kiss. I have never known a connection quite like this one. I am both excited and afraid.

Nothing could hold me back from him. Nothing could change my mind. I am in love with the man I have been searching for. Oddly enough, he found me.

Here I am, sitting in comforts resting place. Soft colours and gentle fabrics lure me into a world of restfulness. Eyes close and bodies touch, reminding of the innocence of love. Just when I think I am dreaming, I hear his voice and I am stirred.

He stands before me, dazzling in his unknown brilliance... luring me with his youthful soul; A soul that shines brightly as he carries on with duties call.

Off white linen drapes him, hiding his much desired form... and still he is unaware. Sometimes he looks up and I watch his eyes soften, secretly wondering what has drawn this man to my life.

His vast wonder intrigues me, an emotion that has escaped me for years. Once again he catches my gaze and I notice again his boyish smile. I can only wonder what days full of pleasure will follow this man.

Here I find myself, consumed in thoughts and surrounded by all things him.

I find myself thinking of him. Then again; then again. Every moment that is filled in idle duty contains a part of him.

There he is, all the time, hiding behind each moments' thought. What lovely thoughts and reminders stem from him.

When all is chaotic, I am left calm. He softens me. He has awakened a light in me, a light that shines brightly and passionately. A light I don't foresee going dim.

The sound of his voice uplifts me. I melt into him like ice in summers alcoholic beverage; diluting a new mixture of tasteful and thirst-quenching wetness.

And what ecstasy this wetness brings; fulfilling and spilling over the capacity of cups brim. When I think of him, I smile… at whatever point I am, at whatever place I am at, at the age I currently find myself.

Every time I feel him it feels like the first time. I lose myself in a sea of emotions, washing away the days before him. I come alive in his presence. His eyes burn into me and awaken me with even the most momentary glance. He represents everything I associate with love.

There is a magic about him that is all his own.

There are few things in life that we can be sure of. Even when we are, it is most times followed by doubt or fear. I can say with conviction, with all the sureness I have today, that he is the best person I have come to know. There is a magic associated with him. The magic that sprinkles 'happy dust' on my life and its current existence.

There are countless words and emotions that I associate with him. There are countless reasons we seem to just fit. To whatever is in the air that seems to be blessing our union, to whatever governs the existence of long standing emotions, to whatever destiny caused our lives to cross paths, I am indebted.

And just like that, the words flow out… at first from mind to conscious thought, and then from conscious thought to words spoken.

The fear associated with professions of love mounting up inside me… fear that ends up as wasted energy as I learn the man I love.

With each new profession of emotion I am left relieved. My love is well received and for the first time, professed with no doubt. I have never known doubtless emotion before I knew him. He renews all hope in trust and intimacy. I always wondered if my professions in the past were truly mine or a means to provide comfort to partners I seemingly loved.

This wonder is no longer. This time my love is sure.

When I look at him, I am at ease. I feel comfortable. Sometimes his look overwhelms me and tears sting my tired eyes… eyes that take in all of his movements; eyes that watch him with desire.

Many times I have to catch myself from mentally going forward and missing the brilliant moment I am sharing with him.

I want to be moving forward and still at the same time. Still, to preserve this perfection, and moving forward to reach a new plateau.

Most times I see him I am overflowing with love; literally bursting with sentiment, filling quiet rooms with murmured professions. When I think of him, the same. When I hear his voice the same; and when I see his picture.

Something about his aura calls to me. He warms me. He reminds me of all things good. Sometimes I am so afraid that I think of how I'd redeem myself if I were wrong about him. Then I remind myself that I am on the wrong path and continue on towards the new and wonderful love.

The intensity of our union is overwhelming. Everything fits; a seemingly perfect match. Perhaps it is not seemingly; perhaps it is actual.

Actual perfection. A fantastic combination of love and reality.

I am in love. Really. In reality. Soulmates do exist.

Here comes the scary part. The part where your life gains a new focus. The part where everything starts to centre around a new being; a united being; him and I.

The realignment of self: To allow this progression is a huge risk. To stop the progression is the beginning of the end. Two lives remain then. The loss of a united front.

So here I am, beginning to see the shift in my life perception. It feels so right. There are moments when I am afraid; panic stricken even; but forward I continue. My life has changed. A new wonderful component has been added and I want to allow for him.

And when I think of him, I smile. He means so much to me. I laugh with him and sometimes I cry to him. He comforts me.

He fills me with strength of emotion. I love him like I have loved no other. I fear life without him like I fear nothing else. A day without him seems so wrong. I miss his smile. I miss his embrace.

I have a soulmate. He is my love.

Days fly by and the future grows near. I often wonder how I got here so fast... followed by the inevitable, "What took me so long?"

Everything seems clearer now. Life issues seem to pale in comparison to the dreams I know will come.

When I dream I think of him. When I run through daily tasks, I think of him. When did he become part of my dreams? Sometimes I think he always was.

What ease in which he fits into each part of my world. Another day draws near to its end. A new day filled with normally accepted routines of chaos; a day I know will end with him.

The countdown to his warmth begins as anticipation grows inside me; similar to the growth of maternal love as child grows in womb; larger as each day passes; stronger as moments pass on.

And when I think of him I smile. Just like that it happens. He brings me happiness.

Eight months have passed. It feels like an eternity... yet has gone by so quickly. How many hours have I spent with him, you ask? Countless.

I don't frighten him with my outward expressions of emotion or frustration. He remains constant through it all. Sometimes I wonder what holds all things together. Other times I just have random thoughts that I record in an attempt to remember the quasi-substance of my life.

My relationship has changed. Somewhere along the way I have begun to depend on him. He warms me. I feel the need to be close to him at the end of a bad day.

He frightens me. Have I ever known what it was like to need? Have I been provided for so well that I never knew what it meant to need more? Then I laugh. I always want more.

The transition has taken place. I am beyond falling in love. I am living in the loving.

The centre core of relationships emotion. A constant force pulling you deeper until you find yourself, unable to think of anyone else. A fixed gaze on one person; and in that gaze a combination of love, hope, desire and passion, fear and apprehension.

But none the less, I am in loving; caught somewhere between beginning and middle, wondering if I could ever feel more.

The love I have found is still the love for me.

I sometimes find myself planting seeds of annoyance, testing the parameters of a love I am sure will not survive; each time I fail.

I look at him and smile. He stays. He always stays. He is the look of love; the look of my love.

I love to write to him. I love to read to him. We have special music that belongs to us; Music that sweeps us into our world.

His eyes beam out at me. He looks over. I look back.

I wish my children to have his eyes. I wish many things.

You are the sun and I am the stars.
By the same token we are as different
As night and day.
When the darkness fades and
The morning comes,
I rest assured knowing you'll brighten tomorrow's skies.
I wish you had the same confidence
In the stars at night.

Chapter 29

*A*ll things change. Even love.

Some may call it growth. Some consider it gradual death; but change it does. A year has passed. I still love him.

My tolerance for trivial issues has decreased. I am getting older. Outside pressures add strain to my current mindset. I am under the weight of chaos's burden.

I am crushed and I am crushing.

Am I willfully hurting the man I love in an attempt to grasp my space? Do I need to regain my strength and release the heaviness of others? Why is it considered cold when you pro-actively take back your own strength for your own well-being?

My love has changed.

It has frustration and resentments. It has anger and impatience. It has harsh words at times. It has expectations and it has a standard… a minimum standard. And this is where the change of love begins… when the mind sets parameters and the heart no longer rules.

This is right; this is not. This is acceptable; this is not. I don't like this, I expect that. The beginning of the gradual murder of beautiful love.

Can I stop? Probably not. Do I want to? Maybe. Will I? Unlikely.

And so it happens… just like that, love has changed. I tolerate less but invest more. I nag but continue to please. I question my feelings and I love him more. I question and I love. I keep loving. I don't love like I used to. I have changed. I am methodical.

The strains of the combination of work and life and love have desensitized me.

I am less me now than I have ever been. I am less me now than I have ever been. I am less me now than I have ever been.

When I feel this way I often let go of any stress that I can. In the past, the only stress or added pressure I could let go of was my boyfriend. I ended relationships when I felt I was losing myself. I don't want to do this again but I can't lose myself either.

When I try to pull back and re-gain the strength that is me, my partner continues to want this strength too. This is the way I am manipulated.

I allow myself to be overextended and then fight to take it back.

Just like this it happens. I am learning my way to my inner self.

I am less me now that I have ever been. I will revisit this.

Chapter 30

*J*ust like that it happened. Love echoed from the sound of a beating heart; the look of love on one knee.

Tears are shed and hearts race. A new life begins here.

I was always afraid of the love that comes with a furthered commitment. I was always afraid of the feelings of constraint. I was always afraid.

But fear I have no longer. He has overtaken me with a tremendous love.

Just like that... a commitment of souls' heart... a depth of something so intense has swept over me. My love for him has exploded.

I look at him and I see him differently. I feel for him differently. Our love has changed. This time it is forever.

The snow fell lightly, landing on cabins peak; a winter wonderland of perfection. Echoes of laughter sliding on the icy coldness of winters' air.

Deep inside a room of warmth were the beating of two hearts; one much louder than the other; a moment of triumph after hours of build-up leading to the joining of hearts.

An embrace so tight marking a new bond of shared dreams; shared dreams of future hopes... the aging of young love.

Wrapped in loves gaze, filled with warmth and sureness, outwardly wanting the wonders of each anticipated year to come.

My love has changed. This time it feels real. I am engaged.

Chapter 31

*A*nd then a nephew is born… small eyes and tiny fingers… an image of perfection in a seemingly imperfect world. A new life begins… not only for him, but for all of us… waiting anxiously to see him again, watch him, learn him… emotions settle upon our beating hearts and love explodes within us. A baby arrives and new lives are born.

I have a nephew. I have never known this depth of love… well for anyone other than my younger brothers. Although, this time it isn't quite the same. I am older now, and each time I happen to lay eyes on him, he is all that exists. He is tiny. He is adorable. He is a piece of the future of our lives existing right here in the present.

I will never forget the first time his eyes opened, his first smile, his first giggle.

What a beautiful new feeling and bond in our family.

I love to hold him. I love to kiss him. I love to tell him I love him.

Wrapped in the warmth and comfort of love, he lays, looking up at the surrounding sounds of the familiar voices of his family; unaware that he is in a room of eight adults who would give their life for him.

He wraps his tiny fingers around mine as I feed him; looks up towards me and rests his tired eyes.

My nephew is an angel. He will be afforded the luxuries that many aunts and uncles can afford.

His tiny little world will grow as we wait in anticipation to applaud his first accomplishments. All this love, and hope, and dream surrounding one child, the moment he entered this world.

My nephew has arrived after what seemed like an eternity. My sister is slowly turning into my mom; doing all the wonderful things only mom's know how to do.

We all watch her. She gave two lives in fifteen months. She may never be canonized, but I think she is a Saint.

Chapter 32

My life has changed. It continues on as it always has. Time goes on, this time with a shift in perception. I am still living differently. This time, the catalyst is not the emotion of pain, but the emotions associated with affection, and all that comes with newfound joy.

The world is still turning. The faces that surround me are still carrying on, unaware of my recent increase in happiness, just as they were unaware of my once increased pain. Love has a similar effect as pain and loss have on my view of existence. Regardless of what anyone may tell me, after meeting my soulmate, the love of my life, my angel, my treasure, my life will never be the same. *(Amore mio, ti amo tanto tesoro)* I am on a new path and I couldn't be happier.

I blinked and I am married. Countless days of chaotic planning leading up to one special day. Here I am married. At whatever age I am, in the dim light of my soon to be old room. I am a fountain of tears, filled with emotion. Almost too much emotion.

The fears of planning such a momentous occasion have melted away and in its place the fear of what the future will bring. Will I find the comfort and security I am hoping for or will I end up sad and lonely like so many other blank faces?

Here I am, in the place I find myself, missing home. With all the craziness home could bring, I never thought I'd miss it until now. I am homesick. I miss the walls, the surrounding love and the faces I've come to associate with home.

I miss my father and my grandmother and 'Jeena.'

Just like that it happens, you get married, and find all the moments, all the places, all the faces you call home. And life goes on… and you start again. Half sure. Half in. All confused. Hope takes its rightful place in your heart and dreams, and expectations of another's on-looking eyes maintain order.

Just like that it happened. I am here. And so is he.

Chapter 33

Something in my soul demands attention. Somewhere deep inside me I am unsettled. I find myself searching for what may never come to surface.

Is it possible that I have a constant desire for more? (There it is again) Am I always searching? Am I settling for less than I want and then asking for more? Am I looking for the same momentum in another that I have in myself? Do we ever find someone who moves at the same pace, in the same direction, or on the same path? Why am I always needing growth? When will I stop?

Just like that it happens. Doubt Lives.

I'm in a new life. Even less me than before. I astound myself, mainly because I am surprised at the ease of letting go of me. I have forgotten my groove, or have lost it. Everything I thought would be is... but not quite the same.

Shadows have been cast upon my dreams.

And so I find myself here at whatever age I am, at whatever stage I'm at. Wondering.

I have never been less me than I am now. Again.

Here I find myself, months before the birth of my magnificence, lost in what I once thought was real.

Somewhere deep inside me I exist. I am loving. I am calm. Layers of age cloak me. The ages of time and the ages of life. There is pain. There is misery, there is brightness and loss. I love from within, circled by marvelous clouds of emotion. I hurt.

Somewhere beneath me I am.

Love does not exist. Love is a fleeting moment randomly placed in a series of consecutive letdowns to give you hope... to help you feel less trauma for having walked into a dream that ended before it began.

And then a gleam of love again and a hint of hope is restored. Each time wishing it won't end the way it inevitably will. In letdown.

And here I am, at my current age, wishing, dreaming, hoping, and knowing. The only love I have is within me. Buried in the watery darkness... yearning to see light.

And so love DOES exist. Just not out here. Not out loud. Not as I thought I knew.

Chapter 34

*J*ust like that it happens. A son is born and so is a mother. A new world. A new meaning. A new life.

He moves with the ease of a feather floating on the wings of air. Gently. Softly. But with purpose. His overwhelming intensity is luring. The love I have for him beams out and lights his path.

He is my heart and every ounce of my love personified into the most beautiful boy. He is my love. He is my Angel. Just like that it happened. He came into my life and added magic and joy and overwhelming love to everything.

I blinked. He grew. A year has passed and each day brings with it another explosion of love and miracles for my son, my angel, my world.

From the moment he was born the intensity of love, inside me, for him, overwhelmed me and seemed to minimize all other emotions I have ever felt or thought I knew.

The love I feel inside me as a mother is the strongest most beautiful pure heartfelt love. There are no words that can describe the power in the love a parent has and experiences for their child.

Every time I look at him I am taken aback by his perfection in my eyes. He is the most beautiful part of me. He is the best of his father and I wrapped into one toddler being.

I am so proud of him. All of his words and sounds and movements. The development of his mind and emotions and imagination are a miracle to be able to experience. His voice gives me peace every time I hear it.

A world without him would end me in one blow. A world without him would not be magnificent. There would be no world without him.

He has created in his life, a new world for me. He has created a new and better and more natural me. I am not sure I existed fully before I was a mother. Surely I never really lived; not in the fullest sense of living.

When I look at M I am filled with love. He is radiant. He is the sun in my skies. He gives me warmth and light and hope. M is immensity. He is larger than anything I have known. He is my salvation. He brings me to life each day; He resurrects me from the pain of life's realities, and guides me to a path of endless joy and love. Here I am, at whatever age I am at, watching my son in absolute and total loving.

So much of who I am came to life when M was born. Just like that it happened. A son was born and a mother came to life.

I should take a moment to mention that 9 days before the birth of my son, my niece was born. She is marvelous and sweet. She is loving. She peers out with her big eyes catching everything in her gaze. She exasperates her loving. She has tightly curled hair and a timid voice but there is a fierce strength in her. She will be mighty. She will change the world.

Chapter 35

Somewhere beneath me I am. Just like that it happened. I woke up. And my marriage ended.

Years of pent up feeling weighs like snow on the roof after a long nights snowstorm; cracking the foundation of comfort's home. Caving in the roof of shelter I've come to rely on.

Tired and weary I see him. Fear stands tall and triumphant before me. It takes all that I am and all that I have to get past him. He crushes me on every front. I am weakened.

Distraught with confused emotions I move forward. The light of a different world lures me forward. A world where I exist. A world where I am loved.

All that I wanted, all that I dreamed of, the image that I called Love ceased to exist in my marriage. The excitement, the planning, the nights and hopes and dreams, all a gateway to the broken heart of my Vision.

A future folded inside me, destroyed in a long drawn out series of blows to my emotion. I have lost a vision of Nothing.

Just like that it happened. I was left with my hopes and my fears. One sweep of life's destruction ball and all falls into place again. Just like that the world goes on. Things continue. Life goes forward. Feelings are lost in a pile of rubble.

Perceptions change. I find old letters, old messages from friends. I read them again (for the second or hundredth time).

They have meaning. I find substance in everything. Even words of youth have depth.

When did life start having such meaning? When did my life change?

I often wonder if the change is in my life or if the change is in me because of life. Perhaps it is a mutual conditioning.

Here I am, at whatever age I am, wherever I find myself, romantically and professionally, reading everything for the first time; seeing the world through new eyes, somehow seeing Life. Real life.

Not all the bells and whistles, but the meat and potatoes of existence. Just like that it happened. I grew up. Again.

Somewhere beneath me I am. It is not often I find myself. I am buried. I was buried.

There are times when the me-ness of who I am beams out like a ray of magnificence from a lighthouse, reminding me of the path home.

The home where I find myself. I am warm and I am comfortable. I am loved and I am loving. I am searching and I am sought.

Just like that it happens. Icicles melt and spring is here again. The ground thaws and the flowers bloom. A new season has begun.

It is so easy to forget who you are when you are faced with a new challenge, on a new path, surrounded by new faces, with new ideas, even if you are missing all that is old.

Every day of new brings revelation of old... how our normal routine makes us jaded, missing all the wonder of every day. Overlooking the privileges of each level of love. Conditioned by our standard of loving... forgetting that all things change.

Love is not the only reminder to appreciate. There is also change.

I am melting. A sea of sadness laps me up and carries me a distance. I am diluted and sunshine randomly catches a glimpse of me floating to an unclear destination. I am dizzy. My mind whirls with thought. Tiny ideas and large emotions mix leaving me warm and light headed.

I am lost. I am living without a dream. And is that really living? I've lost direction.

I am empty. I feel no warmth. The radiance of the sun bouncing off me leaving me cold and bewildered. I have not felt romantic love for what seems like an eternity. I have not felt his love. I am moving beyond it. Wondering if I'll ever need it again. Wondering if I ever did. Wondering if I ever had it. How easily it has slipped away.

The past seems like yesterday. The present day a reminder of a faux pas I never examined. And here I am, much smarter, knowing nothing at all. A sea of experience with so much to learn.

And so I begin again. This time with one eye open.

I will allow myself to be
Consumed with sadness
I will allow myself to feel it
I will recognize my depth
And find comfort in it.
I will allow myself to be happy again.
I will find happiness again.
I will find familiarity in loss.
I will find comfort in the new.
I will allow myself to be.

Chapter 36

I am staring at a blank page of paper; the lines of empty space both exhilarating and frightening. My whole existence is here, being scripted.

Somehow, words have found their home and I am drained of the thoughts that whirl in my mind. Thoughts of past errs that marred my once innocent soul, and thoughts of moments that have kept my life as one of substance.

The very realness of all I am is here for you to read. Most of my days were spent looking for acceptance, and now, clarity has found its way home.

I am looking at the world with a renewed freshness. I am enlightened.

When I think of my future, I find all the dreams I have yet to realize. I feel my desire to truly and fully love and the wonder of the feel of being truly loved.

I long for safety; the comfort and security of knowing that I have reached the ever-sought after assurance that comes with seemingly unattainable love, in its truest form and strength. I want to find the strength to love openly and free from my own ridicule. I look forward to the end of the down-play of my truest heartfelt emotions.

I will doubt less and trust more. I've always wanted to trust myself more fully. I never want to wake up and realize that I have settled.

Mostly, I long to feel, and reciprocate, and dream, and laugh, and imagine. I want to be and to believe.

I look forward to a love beyond appearance, abilities, finance, and potential. I will wake up in the morning appreciating all that I am and all that I have. I will not plan every moment of my life. I won't traumatize myself with constant thought and never-ending mind chatter.

I will have found my light and felt my darkness. I will truly be seen by those who remain part of the world I have created.

My future hope guides my present path... one that, no doubt, will bring me to a renewed sense of meaning and worth.

I am all grown up now. I have suffered many kinds of heartache. The loss of love. The even more terrible loss of loved ones. The fear of losing a loved one. The fear of losing myself. I have had heartbreaking moments in my life. I have experienced splendor.

Still I live on as others did before me. Fear of risk that once blinded me now somewhere in the not-so-distant past.

The veil of insecurity has lifted from once innocent eyes.

I see you as you are. I see past your wounded shield. I reach out and remove your mask with one slight of hand, and touch the frightened features of your face. Features that long to trust as mine do, and always have. Features that soften as your guard comes crashing down.

To trust again...Will I ever? Will I secretly fear as you secretly do?

When I see you, old scars seem to heal.

I long for a new mix of adult comfort; a place where love and companionship reside. It is only there that we can truly see one another. A place where fear is cast aside and our true selves shine.

I always wanted to be close to you. I always wanted more. As time passed, I wrapped myself in insecurities. Clouded emotions kept me from you. Now I stand before you, bare skin drenched with emotion. I call out for you, hoping you will answer.

I can see you so clearly now. You are my future.

He has entered my life and brought apart
all that I made of myself....
Showed me where I want to be... with him...
For he is no longer only an illusion; an
empty space... a lonely walk.
I have dreamed of him all of my life....
And here he is.
My life's wish personified.
I look forward and see my whole future unfold.

The light of your eyes shine on me.
Bringing forth all things true and old.
Marking a new day with rays of joy.
Thoughts of you rest softly like falling leaves on my soul.
The shine of blue.

Chapter 37

I was saved once. A statue of might pulled me from the depth of my sadness. A life ended rescued in the charm of a new beginning. He is softer than I imagined. He is much more intense than I imagined. He is much more intense than I anticipated. He is heated and lustful and full of fire.

With nothing to lose our love grew… almost instantly forming a bond of attachment. Needs were met and a life of loving came to exist.

Fragile feelings emerged and blossomed into a love so strong it is almost unimaginable. It became a love of depth. It became a love of softness. It was the love I always wanted.

I was brought to life again. It was splendor and adult and mutual. There was a sense of belonging that left me wanting more. Frightened and wounded he accepted me. I was allowed to be the imperfect love that I am.

He let me love him. He welcomed me. I was a woman in his arms. I am a woman in his arms.

He reminded me that my love was worth the challenges. He laughed at my eccentricities and reassured me.

He pacified my fears. This is paramount. He pacified my insecurities for the sake of loving. He was my partner. For the first time I was aware of what that meant.

Fear has taught me to doubt him. Love has taught me to trust him. I have come to understand I want to be with him in the most real sense of my being.

Real life is all I want with him. I want to share real life with him. I want to make him dinner and hold him close and allow love to enter my life for the first time since I had my son.

I want to love him openly and without restriction. I want to be alive with him.

B restored my dreams. I am in love with him.

I was in loving with him.

Chapter 38

I am trying to adjust to my new life choices. I am overcome with emotion. The aftermath of the wrecking balls destruction has left me saddened. A family destroyed and dreams lost. I am moving in a new direction, feeling my way through a new less than familiar path. My dreams have returned and with them the reality of what I let go of.

My rationale reminds me that I did not leave the marriage I thought I had. I left a dynamic that would never bring me to the level of love and acceptance I had hoped for. I left a dynamic that was unable to produce healthy love.

Here I am, at whatever age I am, sitting in my new home, trying to rebuild a life. A life that relies less on others, and more on me. I am working on a return to myself.

When I find my way back to me I will be much wiser, but the humanity in me will lead me to err again. Hopefully this time, less catastrophic, less tragic, and less damaging to a once pure soul gone astray.

I've come so far from where I used to be, but I've not yet arrived. My love is distanced and my hopes are soft and weak. The wants of our loving are no longer mutual. My wants have led me to a path of loneliness. A sad realization of a dream possibly not coming true. The dreams that keep tearing me out of my unsure reality leaving destruction and damage in their path. Mostly in my heart.

My heart is hurting and hopeful. My mind tells me to move forward and to push on. My will tells me to be brave and ask for all the loving that I want and need and dream of. My heart tells me I am in love with a man who is afraid of my dreams. I am afraid to climb out on the limb, to take the risk, to face the answer that will inevitably have to come.

I am in love and I am afraid that when faced with our future, he will waiver.

Today I asked for more. Just like that it happened. I stomped my feet and mustered the strength and watched as a face and a look that I know and love changed from love to fear.

Just like that it ended. And so did I.

Chapter 39

*I*t took apart the best pieces of me; the Me I created with him. A Me that was born of hope, sheltered in promises, and raised in love. Here I find myself at whatever age I am, wounded beyond measure.

Like the blade drops on the guillotine's condemned, I am severed. One swift edge splits me.

In the place of a love in motion is a void of anguish that tears me down. Were it not for the strength of the mother in me, and for my precious son, I would cease to exist as I know myself. I would sink to the depth of my devastation and I fear may never have emerged. I would succumb to my pain and allow myself to destruct in a twisted attempt to stop the heartache.

Just like that it happened. I died and my son unknowingly brought me back to life. Thank God for him.

I am distant. I am lost in thought. I am void of a dream and a path and a want. Well, I have many wants… but the wanting of a man… the strong gusts of desire that have carried me through the last few years. They feel dormant. I wonder how I will ever exist again.

I wonder how I will ever find myself and then I thank God again for the blessings of being a mother. The one area of my life that never falters. The ease of love. The purity of mutual intentions and need. The realness that holds me to course and keeps me from going astray.

When I'm not with my son, I see B in everything. I wish for him in every moment of unexpected joy. The sight of his name breaks me and sends my senses whirling in a pain that does not seem to wane.

I am caught between worlds. In sitting with my emotions I am pained. In joys I am yearning and pained. I wish I could shut down the depth of emotion that causes me so much discomfort.

Somewhere not so deep within me I have hope. A hope I wish I had the strength to cast aside. A hope that cannot and will not let go of a love that burns so strong and deep inside me.

Here is where I find myself. Pained. Hopeful. Distraught. Wishing. Wanting. Yearning. Needing. I am everything. But I am not at peace. And today, that is the only place I want to be.

The hardest part of letting go of him is the crippling fear. Fear he is gone forever, and fear that he will come back. Life without him, and life with him again. Fear of the pain that may never go away and the fear that the pain of being without him may linger with me forever. Facing who I am without him when I re-built myself on a foundation of us. And how do I begin again? I feel fragmented. The part of me that is a mother and a colleague remains. I am a daughter, and a sister and an aunt. I am a friend.

The lover in me, the partner and companion in me, feels levelled. I want to be whole again. I am afraid that this part of me that can love so intensely may be gone forever. Maybe it only existed with him.

In the earliest stage of my grief I sat and waited. I hoped he would return to me. I was dreaming of his hands on my face and chest and body. I missed the feel of him beside me and inside me and with me. I still do.

I missed the scent of his skin on mine. I ached for him. I ache for him.

I ache to feel his embrace and his lips and the intensity of his touch. I am waiting for him to find himself and then to find me. I miss his voice and his smile and his hearty laugh. I miss his softness and his fire.

His temper, oh my… but the after loving… oh my. Part of me is dormant without him. I try to feel my way out of this heartache slowly for fear that I may unravel. I feel like I am waiting for him right now, with all of me. And how foolish I feel for hoping. How foolish it is to wait for a man that does not want a life with me.

What a wonderful life it would have been. Through it all his message was conflicting. He was straddling the boundary of life with me and life without me. He struggled with it and I saw it. He assured me that we were meant to be. And now, at the end, his message is clearer than it's ever been. And in this stemmed my most painful revelation.

How difficult it is, at the point of grief I find myself in, to accept that perhaps a love that meant so much to me, meant so much less to him. And that realization breaks me every time it passes through my mind. It drives tears to my eyes and pain to my heart and an ache in the pit of my stomach that feels like it stems from the deepest of my sentiments. It manifests in me. I long to let it go. I wish to let it go. I want to be free of the heartache that overwhelms me any time I think of the love that chose to leave.

Not only did I lose him, but his children. I loved his girls. I miss them. And my son misses them. And I secretly wish I will see them sometime and all the time, throughout my life. I want to know the women they grow up to be. I want to see them as magnificent brides, as loving mothers, and as the women I imagined they would one day be. I wish all the time that there was something in me in the time that I knew them, that for them marked something that they cherished. I wish I could have been witness to the lives they were to lead. I wish so many things. I always have.

If one day I am so lucky that they may find themselves reading this, may the love I have for them radiate out of this page and into their arms and fill them with a glow so bright, and a love so magnificent that it beams the brightest light through all of their fears, and doubts, and insecurities so that they see that in my eyes they are beautiful and perfect and worthy of all things great. If I can see that, the world can.

Girls - Never settle. Never give up. Never lose faith. Always believe in miracles. Always believe in yourself. It is in the greatest strains that we find the greatest strength. Trust you will find the strength because you will. Believe your gut. Trust what you see and not what you hear. If what you see and what you hear don't match, beware. If he loves you, he will move mountains to be with you. If you have a broken heart, feel the sadness. Meet it head on. Allow yourself that. If he judges others, he will one day judge you. Love out loud and take the risk. Be a fool for love. Accept your decisions. Accept your mistakes. This is what makes you unique. This is what makes you, you. It is never too late to make a difference or to follow a new dream. Treat people with equal courtesy. You never know the depth of someone's ability or how wonderful they are. Appearances are limiting. See people. If you make a mistake in public, correct it in the same audience. Don't be afraid to be sorry. We are human. Mistakes are ok. Forgive yourself. The friends who seem closest to you might disappoint you, but when you need someone, you will find support where you least expect it. Those are your true friends. Know always that I love you and that there was a time in my life when I felt just like you.

Chapter 40

*T*here is still a part of me that wishes today will be the day he realizes he cannot exist without my love. And then I feel fear again. Fear of losing him. Fear of loving him. Fear of exposing myself to this crippling sensation of loss again.

Part of me believes there will be a coming together and that it will be forever and we will never be apart again. That is the romantic in me. That is the hope in me that lives on. Crippling me with a vision of a life that may never come to be. But I find solace in this vision.

I created a vision on the base of a promise. I was dreaming. I believed in a dream.

I continue to falter when I create a path on promises that never come to fruition. Actions reveal their true intentions and yet words continue to hypnotize me. I am a victim of my own thoughts of a romanticized life. I'm not sure why so much of my life is based on what I hear when I've learned to trust what I see.

People who are not ready to follow through will not follow through. I know this. I've always known this. And this one quality appears in the earliest stages of relationships. I place much value on words spoken and consider them as light promises. They build a foundation of trust for me. And when there is no follow through it has always been an indication of how easy it would be for a person to knowingly disappoint me.

It is one thing to have unrealistic expectations that you expect a man to live up to. That is just a trap. For you and for him. It's an entirely different issue when a man sets the expectation himself and does not honour it.

Love allows us to overlook these things. Because in loving, there is always hope. There is always trust. There is always belief. And how wonderful loving is.

I remember early words professed when intoxicated with love and passion and newness.

Experience has crushed the innocence of the truest false intentions.

Here I am, at whatever age I am, frightened to face the truth. Frightened to move forward. Frightened to live without his love. Frightened to live without the wonderful feeling of loving him.

So much of our life and of our living is bound by our fears.

I don't know how to explain the depth of pain that I feel. I have ache within my ache. It seems like an endless tunnel of grief. It is as if all my desires for romantic things has disappeared along with my will for intimate loving.

And how intimate our loving was. It was the intimacy that I wanted all of my life and finally attained. Granted it is now over but let me just tell you about its magnificence. Every night that we slept next to each other we held hands. We always touched. One part of our bodies, sleep or awake, always touched. There was a comfortable acceptance and absolutely no judging. At least, I never judged, maybe in hindsight he did. I don't suppose I'll ever know, but I definitely don't know today. And we held each other, really held each other. And the passion was unparalleled. Our eyes met and a fire ignited. All the time. Every time. Our words, soft or heated, always landed us in the same place... well, always landed me in the same place. Forgiveness and loving.

I am hurt beyond measure and my heart keeps sending messages of hope to my hopeful mind that sends my emotions whirling over and over again. I have never felt a loss of love like this before. I am clumsily navigating through the broken parts of what seems like a shipwreck.

I still have visions of him in almost everything. I still have hope. I wish I wouldn't. I wish it would dissipate. I wish it would disappear so that I won't have to face the real end. The end that comes when I have to finally acknowledge he is gone from my romantic life.

And that day has arrived. I must face it.

A brisk abandonment leaves my heart and soul reeling and broken.

I long for peace of mind and heart and soul. I long for a lost dream and a lost love. I long for what I want and cannot have. Peace.

Sundays are the hardest day for me. Waking up without him returns me to the same sharp pain I felt months ago when he first stepped away from my life. This is the day when we felt most like a family. This is the day when I felt the strongest sense of belonging. The day when I didn't have to leave, and work wasn't waiting. It was the one morning a week that we were allowed the privilege of being. The mornings unwound slowly. I made him coffee. We reminded each other that we were in love, and then again, and then again. I found him to be magnificent, especially in those moments of loving. And then afterwards.

From the time I met him we spoke every day. He became my best friend and confidante. He became my sounding board. He became for me all that was missing in my life and all that I wanted in a partnership. He became the man I admired and respected and loved. He became so much to me. And I never anticipated he would not be there.

It shouldn't be this hard. We are programmed as humans to accept loss and to learn to live with it. Aren't we?

I find myself missing him from the instant my thoughts stir, even before my eyes open and I am consciously awake. How does that even happen I wonder?

I feel distressed within myself. My heart aching; my eyes stinging with the coming of fresh tears. The tears that never seem to stop coming.

Every time the ink stains this paper it is for him, to him, with some hope that the words will jump from this page, drift gently to his being, and rest softly on his heart. My soul wishes with every word that I write and with every expression of my aching heart.

The thing about B is that he helped me see myself. He validated me as a woman. He reassured me and restored my faith in love. But not in that I was lovable. That I was capable of loving with the depth that I loved him. As a woman loves a man in its fullest sense. I never thought I'd get past the wounds of my separation but I did. He brought me to new places in myself. He allowed me to be, just as I am. With my faults. And my gifts. He responded to my loving so openly. And he grew in my presence. I grew too. And that growth allowed me to find the areas of myself that I thought were lost forever when I acknowledged defeat in my former life. I dreamed again and I wasn't sure I ever would. In his loving I rediscovered myself. I never thought I'd get back to the woman who believed so strongly in romantic love. But I did. And I owe that to him, and to us. I owe that to the dynamic that allowed me to be free again. And although I wish it never ended as abruptly as it did, I will always be grateful that he was part of my life. A part of me will always belong to him, and the dream of the life I thought we would lead.

In the disappointment of our ending, I found the strength to face my sentiment. The parts of me that were hidden and protected. I had no guard with him. I was never guarded. I was open to all things. I don't think I will ever be closed again. He helped me unlock the parts of my loving that are most beautiful and sincere. He allowed me to see myself through his eyes and in doing that, I accepted myself.

I love him. And I miss him. I want to be with him. He does not know how to fit me into his world. The truth is he shouldn't have to. I should belong. When I think of not fitting in I feel expendable. And no one should feel expendable. I am worthy of being loved deeply. The way I loved him. I cannot pretend I do not want to be with him. I cannot live in fear that his future won't include me. Even knowing this I'm not sure that I am ready to move on. I'm not sure that I am ready to give up. I will believe in him, and in us, until I've exhausted every opportunity to continue. That is who I am. This is how I live without regret.

On Sadie Hawkins Day I called him. (Thank you F.D. for that). It was wonderful to hear his voice. Following the folklore I asked him out for a drink. I never imagined he would come.

We had a wonderful dinner and caught up. We laughed. We cried. We gazed. We shared. For me, all of the feelings were present. And for him it seemed the same. I was in the presence of our loving. We held hands. We hugged. There was an energy between us.

And then he was gone.

Sometimes I think that night was the last night we will ever be as we were. Open, loving, and in loving. He is a different man now and I am a different woman.

The sharp pain in my heart associated with him goes in waves now. Sometimes crashing with vigor and sometimes not present at all. The void is still there. I pray that it will not always be there.

The ache inside myself is buried further beneath me. I will cloak it with the happenings of each new day until I can safely be in a place where I can pretend I have moved past it until the day actually comes that I have.

And then I will be free of the haunting thoughts. And then I will sleep deeply again.

I wonder what will remain of my loving heart when I get past the stage of accepting the loss of a person I believed to be my true love. The person I believe to be my true love.

My love for him is profound. It always was.

Chapter 41

*T*oday I found out that my divorce may be processed this month. I feel like this is a step forward for my life. I think how funny that thought is. We are raised in a foundation of family, and assign such high value to it through our lives, but when the wrecking ball of a failed marriage goes through the tower of our lives, divorce feels like the next step forward. It amazes me that life conditioning has us compromising our fundamentals, and even more amazing than that, that we can recognize our ability to disappoint another person to be true to our self and to our needs.

There was a time during my marriage that I couldn't write. My sentiment was bottled. It was corked with my unhappiness. I never thought I'd write again. I never felt further from myself than I did then. I was not yet aware of how to define what I needed from my marriage, and more importantly, I had yet to learn how to ask for it.

I had three great marriage counselors during that time. They taught me three very important things that I carry with me today.

D taught me to communicate everything to my partner in terms of needs. When your partner consistently does not meet your communicated needs, the decision for your next life choice becomes easier and clearer.

P taught me to allow myself that. To allow myself to feel and grieve and find my way through the most taxing of emotions. He taught me to allow myself what I needed to work through the hard times and to forgive myself for the errors along the way. He encouraged me to give myself the strength to get through and allow myself the weakness to give in.

G said something that I will never forget. He said that people will do anything to make their relationship work, except what they have to. This statement validated for me, one of the things I truly wanted from a partner. A person who followed through.

These three great men helped ease me through the difficult choices that were ahead of me at that time. They helped me make sound decisions that I do not regret. They helped me move forward confidently. For that I will always be grateful.

Many years later an amazing thing happened. I met a wonderful, extremely creative woman. She was happy and light and so human. She encouraged me to write and she supported me when I was pained. She listened to me cry and she made me laugh. Her positive aura reminded me of the long ago wonders that existed in my very own home.

I started reading again. I found myself in my favourite books and I was re-invigorated. My inner voice came back to me and I finally found my words. *Thank you M.S.*

Today I find myself 38. Reading through the pages of my life, I realized something. Some girls dream of marriage their whole lives and I didn't. I wasn't the girl who dreamed of the big white dress or the one magical day. I especially didn't dream of the big white dress.

I dreamed of finding great love. And I did. I found the great love of my son. The great love that comes to you when you become a mother.

I found the great love that led me to my marriage and I found all of the beautiful dreams that I associated with marriage. I survived my marriage ending and all of the chaos that was before today. All the heart breaks, all the work strains, all the losses of those I loved along the way.

I found great love again, in the promise of new love when my marriage ended. I survived losing that love. And an amazing thing is happening. My life is going on. It is different. But I am living. I am happy.

I still believe in love and passion and romance. I look forward to finding intimacy again. Or maybe rekindling it, if fate would give me that pleasure.

Maybe I am one of the lucky ones. Even without more.

Just like that it happened. I woke up and felt a return to self. I am not close to being whole again. I'm not sure I will ever be the same.

But I am me. I am intact. I am functioning. I am writing.

I am not yet at peace but I want to be. I am not yet healed. But I will find my way.

And so I begin again…A new path to a hopefully truer happiness.

And so it continues. Just like that it happens.

I have arrived, and what's more, you are there.

Printed in the United States
By Bookmasters